PROFILES OF
Malcolm Baldrige Award Winners

ALLYN AND BACON
Boston • London • Sydney • Toronto • Tokyo • Singapore

This book is published by Allyn & Bacon
A Division of Simon & Schuster
160 Gould Street
Needham Heights, Massachusetts 02194

This book is also published under the title
Award Winning Quality: Strategies from the Winners of the Malcolm Baldrige National Quality Award

ISBN 0-205-14802-6

Printed in the United States of America

10 9 8 7 6 5 4 3 2 1   97 96 95 94 93 92

About BBP
BBP is a division of the Business and Professional Group of Simon & Schuster, a Paramount Communications Company. All of our companies and divisions are leaders in their fields—Prentice Hall in college texts, and professional business & legal services; J.K. Lasser for personal tax planning; Silver Burdett & Ginn in basic reading skills and education; and BBP in multimedia management, supervisory and employee training, to name but a few.

Serving your needs is the largest, most skilled staff of editors, authors, business experts and education specialists ever assembled to bring you the most effective information and training available anywhere. We use the latest technologies to interchange this information so that when you use any of our services you use all of our services—you have access to the united strength and resources of the entire group. You will never find a more dedicated or more technically skilled organization in which to entrust your critical training needs.

BBP, 24 Rope Ferry Road, Waterford, CT 06386

Table of Contents

Chapter Five

Malcolm Baldrige National Quality Award Winners—1991

Chapter Six

Quality Improvement the Baldrige Way: Even Without the Trophy, Your Company Can Become a Winner!

Conclusion

The Bottom Line: Continuous Improvement Is What Counts

Introduction

The Malcolm Baldrige National Quality Award: A Blueprint for Excellence

"An act to amend the Stevenson-Wydler Technology Innovation Act of 1980, to establish the Malcolm Baldrige National Quality Award with the objective of encouraging American business and other organizations to practice effective quality control in the provision of their goods and services."

That brief paragraph has resulted in nothing less than a quality revolution among United States businesses. As the Japanese challenge of the 1980s spurred U.S. companies to focus their attention on quality improvement, the Malcolm Baldrige National Quality Award is generating similar enthusiasm in the 1990s—and it's providing just the blueprint that companies need to define quality for their organizations, involve all personnel in the quality effort, continuously improve their processes and, above all, keep their customers satisfied.

As a quality professional, you've probably been hearing about this prestigious award for some time. You and your company may have even taken part in the application process. Whatever your degree of familiarity with the Baldrige Award, you'll benefit greatly from the information in this book, *Award Winning Quality*.

Chapter One begins with some background information on the Baldrige Award, provided by the people who know best—Award administrators from the National Institute of Standards and Technology (NIST). These experts provide pertinent information about the Award in an easy-to-read question-and-answer format. Following this Q&A session is a presentation of the Baldrige Award criteria, along with helpful scoring guidelines.

Next, you'll get a close-up, *insider's* look at the strategies that have helped Baldrige recipients become quality leaders—*and* award winners. Chapters are arranged in a year-by-year format, beginning with the first year the Baldrige Award was presented, in 1988.

In **Chapter Two**, you'll learn how the first Baldrige winner in the small business category, Globe Metallurgical Inc., teamed up with its customers to promote excellence within its own company. You'll see how Motorola, Inc.'s Six Sigma defect reduction plan and Quality System Review teams are helping it to establish and achieve stringent quality goals. In addition, you'll find out about Westinghouse Electric Corporation's Twelve Conditions of Excellence—all-encompassing imperatives that are enabling this third

1988 Award-winner to achieve excellence throughout its organization.

In **Chapter Three**, Xerox Corporation, a 1989 winner, shares its Leadership Through Quality process and describes, step-by-step, the painstaking strategy it followed in its successful quest for the Baldrige Award. Also, you'll get a glimpse of Milliken & Company's team-based Pursuit of Excellence plan.

Chapter Four discloses how Cadillac Motor Car Company used a Simultaneous Engineering Pyramid to involve everyone from customers, automobile dealers, to operators in assuring a quality product—a plan that helped turn the company around and make it a Baldrige winner in 1990. Federal Express, the first winner in the Service category, shares how it used a Baldrige-based self-improvement plan and twelve quality indicators to deliver top-notch service to its customers. IBM Rochester provides an overview of its decade-long improvement effort. Then, The Wallace Company, the fourth 1990 Award recipient, relates its remarkable success story, detailing how it dug in its heels, made a total quality turnaround in an extremely difficult economic climate, and beat the odds.

Award Winning Quality

Chapter Five covers the 1991 Award winners. First, you'll get an in-depth look at Marlow Industries' Total Quality Management process, and then follow the company through the steps it took in pursuit of the Baldrige Award, learning some tips for application success along the way. Next, Solectron Corporation shares how it blends customer involvement and thorough staff training to build a work environment that encourages a quality-first attitude. Finally, Zytec Corporation discloses the management-by-planning strategy it uses to set quality goals and keep them on track.

These Baldrige success stories are instructional and inspirational reading for any quality professional. They bring home the message that qualifying for the Award is not a matter of good luck, "knowing the right people," or engaging in some fancy sleight-of-hand: It is the result of *making a total commitment to quality and customer satisfaction,* designing a comprehensive quality plan, and then putting out considerable effort—often for many years—to assure excellence throughout every phase of an organization. And then, of course, it's also a matter of going through the rigorous application process itself, which can be grueling for even the most effective organization.

While most companies regard the Baldrige Award as extremely desirable indeed, some may shy away from the application process because they fear that they have not yet reached the level of excellence achieved by these past winners. They may think, "Our quality processes have a long way to go—why should we bother applying for the Award when we know we can't possibly win?"

However, as such Baldrige winners as Marlow Industries, Federal Express, and Xerox know, the true value of the Baldrige application process lies not with winning the Award itself, but with the learning experience that the process can afford a company. So with this in mind, many smart firms across the country—such as AT&T, Preston Trucking Company, The Perkin-Elmer Corporation, and Texas Instruments—are putting the Baldrige process to work as an ongoing quality improvement tool. In **Chapter Six**, you'll learn how these leading companies—and others—are utilizing the Baldrige process to better their organizations, with highly effective results. And you'll gain ideas for doing the same at *your own* company to promote excellence, satisfy your customers, and sharpen your competitive edge.

Chapter One

**An In-Depth Look at the Baldrige Award:
What Does It Take to Be a Winner?**

A Baldrige Q & A Session

How did the Malcolm Baldrige National Quality Award come into existence? Who is eligible to apply? This Chapter addresses the questions of those who are just becoming interested in the Award, while providing Baldrige "veterans" with new insights from the best possible source: two of the Award administrators, who provide pertinent information in a question-and-answer session. Following the Q & A, you'll get a firsthand look at the latest Award criteria.

Q: What is the Malcolm Baldrige National Quality Award, and why was it created?

A: Created by public law as an amendment to the Stevenson-Wydler Act and named for the late Secretary of Commerce, the Malcolm Baldrige National Quality Award is the highest level of national recognition for quality that a United States company can achieve. "The purpose of Stevenson-Wydler was to promote the transfer of federally developed technology to the private sector," explains Dr. Robert Chapman, senior economist, Office of Quality Programs, National Institute of Standards and Technology (NIST) (Gaithersburg, MD).

Building an active partnership between the private sector and the government is fundamental to the Award's success at sparking quality improvement. The Foundation for the Malcolm Baldrige National Quality Award was created to foster such partnerships. One of its objectives is to raise funds to establish an endowment that, when supplemented by fees from Award applicants, will permanently fund the Award program.

Q: Who manages the Award program?

A: Responsibility for managing the Award rests with NIST, a branch of the Department of Commerce. NIST aids U.S. industry through research and services designed to contribute to technology development, technology utilization, and public health and safety. Note: In 1991, NIST awarded the American Society for Quality Control (ASQC) a contract naming the Society administrator of the Award.

Q: Who is eligible to win the Award?

A: Any for-profit business in the United States or its territories may apply. National, state, and local government agencies, not-for-profit organizations, trade associations, and professional societies are not eligible.

Q: Should my company request a Baldrige Award application even if we have no intention of submitting it?

A: Absolutely. In fact, only a small fraction of businesses requesting applications actually submit them to NIST for consideration. (In 1991, for example, approximately 235,000 applications were requested but only 106 were actually submitted.) Most companies use the Award criteria as a "quality blueprint" to improve their quality to the point that they are as competitive as possible in the marketplace (see Chapter 6 for a look at some of these companies). That is, by not focusing on results—but on the conditions and processes that lead to results—the examination offers a framework that can be used to tailor a company's systems and processes toward ever-improving quality performance.

"Many companies have found, after reviewing the examination, that they may have some gaps in their processes and systems that prevent them from getting the biggest bang for their buck," points out Dr. Curt Reimann, association director for Quality Programs at NIST. "For example, they may be training their people but not evaluating or reinforcing that training." The Baldrige criteria highlight the need for these additional activities.

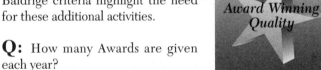

Q: How many Awards are given each year?

A: The Act allows for up to two Awards in each of three categories: Manufacturing, Service, and Small Business (defined as a complete business with not more than 500 full-time employees). However, the standards for winning the Award are absolute, not relative. That means that all winners must meet certain strict criteria, even if it means that fewer than six Awards are given that year.

Q: Why has the Baldrige Award become so popular with United States businesses?

A: "The Award came around at the right time because there is a strong interest in international competitiveness," replies Dr. Reimann. Also, since companies are encouraged to use application guidelines as self-assessment tools, thousands of firms are finding that quality is being "demystified" for them. "They see how they can take quality from a process-driven discipline to a customer-driven discipline," he explains.

"Professional managers who have no background in quality can study our documents and see what quality is all about," Dr. Reimann adds. Also, since the examination team consists of highly respected quality professionals chosen from a broad constituency, companies respect their recommendations.

Finally, one of the requirements for Award winners is to tell other companies how they accomplished their goal so that others may learn from example and improve their quality. "The winners have taken on this requirement as a crusade," Dr. Reimann notes. "As a result, word of the Baldrige Award is spreading throughout the business world."

Q: Who are the examiners, and how are they chosen?

A: Each fall, NIST recruits new examiners. These are quality professionals from around the nation who apply for positions on the Board of Examiners. A board at NIST studies the applicants' qualifications and selects those who meet the highest standards of professionalism, qualification, and peer recognition.

"We try to seek a balance from among a number of different national constituencies," says Dr. Chapman. These constituencies include industry, professional and trade associations, universities, healthcare organizations, and government agencies. Those ultimately selected must participate in a preparation program based on the criteria, the scoring system, and the examination process.

Q: What is covered in the Baldrige Award examination?

A: The examination addresses seven areas: Leadership, Information and Analysis, Strategic Quality Planning, Human Resource Development and Management, Management of Process Quality, Quality and Operational Results, and Customer Focus and Satisfaction. In addition, each of these categories has several subcategories.

The examination is built on a number of key concepts that underlie all requirements included in the examination items. Here is a look at some of these concepts:

➤ *Quality is defined by the customer.*

➤ *The senior leaderships of businesses need to create clear quality values and build those values into the way the company operates.*

➤ *Quality excellence derives from well-designed and well-executed systems and processes.*

➤ *Continuous improvement must be part of the management of all systems and processes.*

➤ *Companies need to develop goals, as well as strategic and operational plans, to achieve quality leadership.*

➤ *Shortening the response time of all company operations and processes needs to be part of the quality improvement effort.*

➤ *Operations and decisions of the company need to be based upon facts and data.*

➤ *All employees must be trained, developed, and involved in all quality activities.*

➤ *Design quality and defect-and-error prevention should be major elements of the quality system.*

➤ *Companies need to communicate quality requirements to suppliers and work to elevate supplier quality performance.*

Q: How is the selection process handled?

A: There are four steps in the Application Review Process:

■ **First-Stage Review.** Several members of the Board of Examiners review each application. Then, a Panel of Judges from the Board determines which applications should proceed to the second stage.

■ **Consensus Review.** At least four members of the Board of Examiners, plus a Senior Examiner, review each application. Again, the Panel of Judges decides which applications will be passed on to the third stage.

■ **Site-Visit Review.** At least five members of the Board of Examiners, plus a Senior Examiner, conduct a three- to four-day on-site verification visit of each applicant that has made it to this stage. The team develops a report for the Panel of Judges. The primary objectives of the site visit are to verify information provided in the application and to clarify issues or questions raised during the review process. The examiners provide the applicant with a site-visit agenda at least two weeks in advance.

■ **Judges' Final Review.** The Panel of Judges conducts a final review of all evaluation reports and then recommends Award recipients to NIST. NIST, in turn, presents the Judges' recommendations to the Secretary of Commerce. Following each year's Award cycle, all applicants receive detailed Feedback Reports that provide information on the strengths and weaknesses found. As part of the report, each applicant receives a profile of how it did in the overall process.

Q: What are the specific criteria for scoring?

A: The system for scoring Examination Items is based on the following three evaluation dimensions:

- **Approach**—the methods the company uses to achieve the purposes addressed in the Examination Items.

- **Deployment**—the extent to which the approaches are applied to all relevant areas and activities addressed and implied in the Examination Items.

- **Results**—the outcomes and effects of achieving the purposes addressed and implied in the Examination Items. (For more specific information on the Scoring Guidelines, see Figure 1-1.)

Q: What fees are involved?

A: Here is the schedule of fees for 1992:

✔ **Eligibility Determination Fee:** $50

✔ **Written Application Review Fee:**
In the Manufacturing Category: $4,000
In the Service Category: $4,000
In the Small Business Category: $1,200
(*Note:* There is also a fee of $1,500 for a supplemental application section. This section must be filed by applicants that are units of companies that are in essentially different businesses.)

✔ **Site-Visit Review Fees:** Paid only by those applicants reaching this stage, these vary, depending on such factors as the number of examiners present and the length of the visit.

Incidentally, the entire Baldrige Award program is funded by these fees, along with additional support from the Foundation mentioned earlier; there is no funding from the United States Government.

Q: What will my company be required to do if it wins the Baldrige Award?

A: Winners are asked to share with other companies their expertise and experiences related to successful quality strategies. However, "winners certainly can't possibly honor every request they receive for information," Dr. Reimann acknowledges. Past experience has proven that Baldrige-winning companies may become bombarded with an overwhelming number of requests for information, so many limit their sharing activities to the annual Quest for Excellence quality conference in Washington, D.C. Others may also schedule "visitors' days" or on-site seminars during the year that representatives from other interested companies may attend.

Q: How do I get more information on the Baldrige Award?

A: Write to: Malcolm Baldrige National Quality Award, National Institute of Standards and Technology, Administration Building, Room A537, Gaithersburg, MD 20899. You may also telephone (301) 975-2036 or FAX (301) 948-3716.

SCORING GUIDELINES

SCORE	APPROACH	DEPLOYMENT	RESULTS
0%	■ anecdotal, no system evident	■ anecdotal	■ anecdotal
10-40%	■ beginnings of systematic prevention basis	■ some to many major areas of business	■ some positive trends in the areas deployed
50%	■ sound, systematic prevention basis that includes evaluation/ improvement cycles ■ some evidence of integration	■ most major areas of business ■ some support areas	■ positive trends in most major areas ■ some evidence that results are caused by approach
60-90%	■ sound, systematic prevention basis with evidence of refinement through evaluation/ improvement cycles ■ good integration	■ major areas of business ■ from some to many support areas	■ good to excellent in major areas ■ positive trends—from some to many support areas ■ evidence that results are caused by approach
100%	■ sound, systematic prevention basis refined through evaluation/improvement cycles ■ excellent integration	■ major areas and support areas ■ all operations	■ excellent (world-class) results in major areas ■ good to excellent in support areas ■ sustained results ■ results clearly caused by approach

Figure 1-1: Scoring Guidelines

MALCOLM BALDRIGE NATIONAL QUALITY AWARD CRITERIA (1992)

INTRODUCTION

The Malcolm Baldrige National Quality Award is an annual Award to recognize U.S. companies that excel in quality management and quality achievement.

The Award promotes:

■ awareness of quality as an increasingly important element in competitiveness,

■ understanding of the requirements for quality excellence, and

■ sharing of information on successful quality strategies and the benefits derived from implementation of these strategies.

Award Participation

The Award has three eligibility categories:

■ Manufacturing companies

■ Service companies

■ Small businesses

Up to two Awards may be given in each category each year. Award recipients may publicize and advertise their Awards. In addition to publicizing the receipt of the Award, recipients are expected to share information about their successful quality strategies with other U.S. organizations.

Companies participating in the Award process submit applications that include completion of the Award Examination.

Award Examination Review

The Award Examination is based upon quality excellence criteria through a public-private partnership. In responding to these criteria, each applicant is expected to provide information and data on the company's quality processes and quality improvement. Information and data submitted must be adequate to demonstrate that the applicant's approaches could be replicated or adapted by other companies.

The Award Examination is designed not only to serve as a reliable basis for making Awards but also to permit a diagnosis of each applicant's overall quality management.

All applications are reviewed and evaluated by members of the Malcolm Baldrige National Quality Award Board of Examiners. When Board members are assigned to review applications, business and quality expertise is matched to the business of the applicant. Accordingly, applications from manufacturing companies are assigned primarily to Board members with manufacturing expertise, and service company applications are assigned primarily to those with service expertise. Strict rules regarding real and potential conflicts of interest are followed in assigning Board members to review applications.

Applications are reviewed without funding from the United States Government. Review expenses are paid primarily through application fees; partial support for the reviews is provided by the Foundation for the Malcolm Baldrige National Quality Award.

After the Award Examination review, all applicants receive feedback reports prepared by members of the Board of Examiners.

Purpose of This Document

This document contains the Award Criteria, a description of the Criteria, scoring guidelines, and other information. In addition to serving as a basis for submitting an Award application, the material contained in this document helps provide a basis for self-assessment, planning, training, and other uses by any organization.

DESCRIPTION OF THE AWARD CRITERIA (1992)

Award Criteria Purposes

The Malcolm Baldrige National Quality Award Criteria are the basis for making Awards and providing feedback to applicants. In addition, they have three other important national purposes:

■ to help elevate quality standards and expectations;

■ to facilitate communication and sharing among and within organizations of all types based upon common understanding of key quality requirements; and

■ to serve as a working tool for planning, training, assessment, and other uses.

The Award Criteria are directed toward dual results-oriented goals: To project key requirements for delivering ever-improving value to customers while at the same time maximizing the overall productivity and effectiveness of the delivering organization.

To achieve these results-oriented goals, the Criteria need to be built upon a set of values that together address and integrate the overall customer and company performance requirements.

Core Values and Concepts

The Award Criteria are built upon these core values and concepts:

■ Customer-driven quality

■ Leadership

■ Continuous improvement

■ Full participation

■ Fast response

■ Design quality and prevention

■ Long-range outlook

■ Management by fact

■ Partnership development

■ Public responsibility

[Note:] Brief descriptions of the core values and concepts follow.

Customer-Driven Quality

Quality is judged by the customer. All product and service attributes that contribute value to the customer and lead to customer satisfaction and preference must be addressed appropriately in quality systems. Value, satisfaction, and preference may be influenced by many factors throughout the customer's overall purchase, ownership, and service experiences. This includes the relationship between the company and customers—the trust and confidence in products and services—that leads to loyalty and preference. This concept of quality includes not only the product and service attributes that meet basic requirements. It also includes those that enhance them and differentiate them from competing offerings. Such enhancement and differentiation may include new offerings, as well as unique product-product, service-service, or product-service combinations.

Customer-driven quality is thus a strategic concept. It is directed toward market share gain and customer retention. It demands constant sensitivity to emerging customer and market requirements and measurement of the factors that drive customer satisfaction. It also demands awareness of developments in technology, and rapid and flexible response to customer and market requirements. Such requirements extend well beyond defect and error reduction, merely meeting specifications, or reducing complaints. Nevertheless, defect and error reduction and elimination of causes of dissatisfaction contribute significantly to the customers' view of quality and are thus also important parts of customer-driven quality. In addition, the company's approach to recovering from defects and errors is crucial to its improving both quality and relationships with customers.

Leadership

A company's senior leaders must create clear and visible quality values and high expectations. Reinforcement of the values and expectations requires their substantial personal commitment and involvement. The leaders must take part in the creation of strategies, systems, and methods for achieving excellence. The systems and methods need to guide all activities and decisions of the company and encourage participation and creativity by all employees. Through their regular personal involvement in visible activities, such as planning, review of company quality performance, and recognizing employees for quality achievement, the senior leaders serve as role models reinforcing the values and encouraging leadership in all levels of management.

Continuous Improvement

Achieving the highest levels of quality competitiveness requires a well-defined and well-executed approach to continuous improvement. Such improvement needs to be part of all operations and of all work unit activities of a company. Improvements may be of several types: (1) enhancing value to the customer through new and improved products and services; (2) reducing errors, defects, and waste; (3) improving responsiveness and cycle time performance; and (4) improving productivity and effectiveness in the use of all resources. Thus, improvement is driven not only by the objective to provide better quality, but also by the need to be responsive and efficient—both conferring additional marketplace advantages. To meet all of these objectives, the process of continuous improvement must contain regular cycles of planning, execution, and evaluation. This requires a basis—preferably a quantitative basis—for assessing progress, and for deriving information for future cycles of improvement.

Full Participation

Meeting the company's quality and performance objectives requires a fully committed, well-trained, and involved work force. Reward and recognition systems need to reinforce full participation in company quality objectives. Factors bearing upon the safety, health, well-being, and morale of employees need to be part of the continuous improvement objectives and activities of the company. Employees need education and training in quality skills related to performing their work and to understanding and solving quality-related problems. Training should be reinforced through on-the-job applications of learning, involvement, and empowerment. Increasingly, training and participation need to be tailored to a more diverse work force.

Fast Response

Success in competitive markets increasingly demands ever-shorter product and service introduction cycles and more rapid response to customers. Indeed, fast response itself is often a major quality attribute. Reduction in cycle times and rapid response to customers can occur when work processes are designed to meet both quality and response goals. Accordingly, response time improvement should be included as a major focus within all quality improvement processes of work units. This requires that all designs, objectives, and work unit activities include measurement of cycle time and responsiveness. Major improvements in response time may require work processes and paths to be simplified and shortened. Response time improvements often "drive" simultaneous improvements in quality and productivity. Hence it is highly beneficial to consider response time, quality, and productivity objectives together.

Design Quality and Prevention

Quality systems should place strong emphasis on design quality—problem prevention achieved though building quality into products and services and into the processes through which they are produced. Excellent design quality may lead to major reductions in "downstream" waste, problems, and associated costs. Design quality includes the creation of fault-tolerant (robust) processes and products. A major design issue is the design-to-introduction cycle time. To meet the demands of ever-more rapidly changing markets, companies need to focus increasingly on shorter product and service introduction times. Consistent with the theme of design quality and prevention, continuous improvement and corrective actions need to emphasize interventions "upstream"—at the earliest stages in processes. This approach yields the maximum overall benefits of improvements and corrections. Such upstream intervention also needs to take into account the company's suppliers.

Long-Range Outlook

Achieving quality and market leadership requires a future orientation and long-term commitments to customers, employees, stockholders, and suppliers. Strategies, plans, and resource allocations need to reflect these commitments and address training, employee development, supplier development, technology evolution, and other factors that bear upon quality. A key part of the long-term commitment is regular review and assessment of progress relative to long-term plans.

Management by Fact

Meeting quality and performance goals of the company requires that process management be based upon reliable information, data, and analysis. Facts and data needed for quality assessment and quality improvement are of many types, including: customer, product and service performance, operations, market, competitive comparisons, supplier, employee-related, and cost and financial. Analysis refers to the process of extracting larger meaning from data to support evaluation and decision making at various levels within the company. Such analysis may entail using data individually or in combination to reveal information—such as trends, projections, and cause and effect—that might not be evident without analysis. Facts, data, and analysis support a variety of company purposes, such as planning, reviewing company performance, improving operations, and comparing company quality performance with competitors'.

A major consideration relating to use of data and analysis to improve competitive performance involves the creation and use of performance indicators. Performance indicators are measurable characteristics of products, services, processes, and operations the company uses to evaluate performance and to track progress. The indicators should be selected to best represent the factors that determine customer satisfaction and operational performance. A system of indicators tied to customer and/or company performance requirements represents a clear and objective basis for aligning all activities of the company toward common goals. Through the analysis of data obtained in the tracking processes, the indicators themselves may be evaluated and changed. For example, indicators selected to measure product and service quality may be judged by how well they correlate with customer satisfaction.

Partnership Development

Companies should seek to build internal and external partnerships, serving mutual and larger community interests. Such partnerships might include those that promote labor-management cooperation with suppliers and customers, and linkages with education organizations. Partnerships should consider longer-term objectives as well as short-term needs, thereby creating a basis for mutual investments. The building of partnerships should address means of regular communication, approaches to evaluating progress, means for modifying objectives, and methods to accommodate to changing conditions.

Public Responsibility

A company's customer requirements and quality system objectives should address areas of corporate citizenship and responsibility. These include business ethics, public health and safety, environment, and sharing of quality-related information in the company's business and geographic communities. Health, safety, and environmental considerations need to take into account the life cycle of products and services and include factors such as waste generation. Quality planning in such cases should address adverse contingencies that may arise throughout the life cycle of production, distribution, and use of products. Plans should include problem avoidance and company response if avoidance fails, including how to maintain public trust and confidence. Inclusion of public responsibility areas within a quality system means not only meeting all local, state, and federal legal and regulatory requirements, but also treating these and related requirements as areas for continuous improvement. In addition, companies should support—within reasonable limits of their resources—national, industry, trade, and community activities to share nonproprietary quality-related information.

Criteria Framework

The core values and concepts are embodied in seven categories, as follows:

1.0 Leadership

2.0 Information and Analysis

3.0 Strategic Quality Planning

4.0 Human Resource Development and Management

5.0 Management of Process Quality

6.0 Quality and Operational Results

7.0 Customer Focus and Satisfaction

The framework connecting and integrating the categories is given in [Figure 1-2 on the following page].

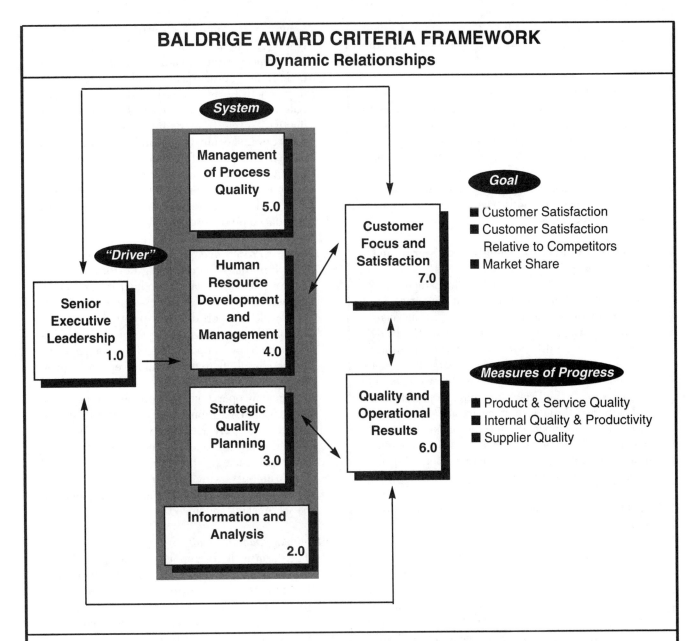

Figure 1-2: Baldrige Award Criteria Framework

The framework has four basic elements:

Driver
Senior executive leadership creates the values, goals, and systems, and guides the sustained pursuit of quality and performance objectives.

System
System comprises the set of well-defined and well-designed processes for meeting the company's quality and performance requirements.

Measures of Progress
Measures of progress provide a results-oriented basis for channeling actions to delivering ever-improving customer value and company performance.

Goal
The basic aim of the quality process is the delivery of ever-improving value to customers.

The seven Criteria categories shown in the figure are further subdivided into Examination Items and Areas to Address. These are described below.

Examination Items
In all, there are 28 Examination Items among the seven Examination Categories. Examination Categories each contain two or more Examination Items. Each item focuses on a major element of an effective quality system. All information submitted by applicants is in response to the specific requirements given within these items. Each item is assigned an

Examination point value. Item titles and point values are enumerated [in Figure 1-3; see the end of the Chapter].

Areas to Address

Each Examination Item includes a set of Areas to Address (Areas). The Areas serve to illustrate and clarify the intent of the items and to place limits on the types and amounts of information the applicant should provide. Areas are not assigned individual point values, because their relative importance depends upon factors such as the applicant's type and size of business and quality system.

The Pivotal Role of the Quality and Operational Results Category

The Quality and Operational Results Category (6.0) plays a central role in the Award Criteria. This Category provides a focus and purpose for all quality system actions. In addition, it represents the bridge between the quality system and the customer. Through this focus, the dual purpose of quality—superior value of offerings as viewed by the customer and the marketplace, and superior company performance as determined through productivity and effectiveness indicators—is maintained. The other major purpose of Category 6.0 is to provide key information (measures of progress) for evaluation and improvement of quality system processes and practices.

The Quality and Operational Results Category consists of four items:

6.1 Product and Service Quality Results

This item calls for reporting quality levels and improvements for key product and service attributes—attributes that truly matter to the customer and to the marketplace. These attributes are derived from customer-related items ("listing posts") which make up Category 7.0. If the attributes have been properly selected, improvements in them should show a strong positive correlation with customer and marketplace improvement indicators—captured in Items 7.4 and 7.5. The correlation between quality and customer indicators is a critical management tool. It is a device for focusing on key attributes. In addition, the correlation may reveal emerging or changing market segments or changing importance of attributes.

6.2 Company Operational Results

This item calls for reporting performance and improvements in quality and productivity of the company. Paralleling Item 6.1, which focuses on attributes that matter to the customer, Item 6.2 focuses on attributes that best reflect overall com-

pany performance. Such attributes are of two types: (1) generic—common to all companies; and (2) business-specific. Generic attributes include cycle time, internal quality, and those that relate to productivity, as reflected in use of labor, materials, energy, capital, and assets. Indicators of productivity, cycle time, or internal quality should reflect overall company performance. Business- or company-specific effectiveness indicators vary greatly and may include indicators such as rates of invention, environmental quality, export levels, new markets, and percent of sales from recently introduced products or services.

6.3 Business Process and Support Service Results

This item calls for reporting performance and improvements in quality, productivity, and effectiveness of the business processes and support services which support the principal product and service production activities. This permits a demonstration of how support units of the company link to and contribute to overall improvement in quality (reported in Item 6.1) and overall improvement in company operational performance (reported in Item 6.2). This item is thus a useful device in aligning support activities with the company's overall principal quality, productivity, and business objectives. Through this item, special requirements, which differ from work unit to work unit and define work-unit effectiveness, can be set, tracked, and linked to one another.

6.4 Supplier Quality Results

This item calls for reporting quality levels and improvements in key indicators of supplier quality. The term "supplier" refers to external providers of products and services, "upstream" and/or "downstream" from the company. The focus should be on the most critical quality attributes from the point of view of the company—the buyer of the products and services. Trends and levels of quality should reflect results by whatever means they occur—via improvements by suppliers within the supply base, through changes in selection of suppliers, or both.

Key Characteristics of The Award Criteria

1. The Criteria are directed toward producing results.

The values outlined above are directed toward the results-oriented goals of the Criteria. Results, as used in the Criteria, are a composite of key performance areas:

■ customer satisfaction

- customer satisfaction relative to competitors

- market share

- customer indicators such as complaints and customer retention

- market responsiveness and cycle time

- product and service quality

- internal quality, productivity, waste reduction, and asset utilization

- company-specific effectiveness indicators such as new markets, new technology, and new products

- supplier quality and supplier development

- environmental quality, occupational safety and health, and regulatory compliance

- employee development, well-being, and satisfaction

- contributions to national and community well-being

Assessment of these results is based upon one or more of three factors: (1) improvement trends; (2) current levels; and (3) benchmarks, evaluations, and other comparisons that establish levels and trends relative to the performance of others, especially appropriately selected leaders.

2. The Criteria are nonprescriptive.

The Criteria represent an integrated set of requirements incorporating the ten core values described above. However, the Criteria do not prescribe how the core values are to be implemented in a particular company. Specifically, they do not prescribe:

- company organization

- quality organization, if any (The seven categories of the Criteria do not necessarily correspond to departments or company units.)

- specific quality techniques

- type of quality system

- method of quality system implementation

- technologies to be used

The Criteria are nonprescriptive for [the following]

two important reasons:

(1) Organizations, techniques, and technologies vary greatly among businesses, depending on business size, type, and other factors.

(2) By focusing on requirements, companies are encouraged to develop unique, creative, or adaptive overall approaches to achieving the goals of the Criteria.

3. The Criteria link process to results.

The Award Criteria provide a link between processes and results, as described above in the Pivotal Role of the Quality and Operational Results Category. Integration in the Criteria is achieved through many direct and indirect relationships and linkages among the requirements. In addition, many parts of the Criteria call for aggregation and assessment of unit-level and company-level performance, thus encouraging an integrated view of all activities.

4. The Criteria are part of a diagnostic system.

The Criteria and the scoring system make up a two-part diagnostic system. The Criteria focus on requirements. The scoring system focuses on the factors that should be used in assessing strengths and areas for improvement. Together the two parts of the diagnostic system direct attention to activities that contribute to reaching the goals of the Criteria.

5. The Criteria are comprehensive.

The requirements contained in the Criteria cover all operations, processes, and work units of the company. In addition, the Criteria support business strategy and business decisions and pertain to all transactions, including those related to fulfilling public responsibilities.

6. The Criteria include key learning cycles.

The arrows in [Figure 1-2] denote linkage and dynamic relationships and feedback among the framework elements. The primary dynamic characteristic of the Criteria is their inclusion of cycles of continuous improvement. These cycles of learning, adaptation, and improvement are explicit and implicit in every part of the Criteria. The cycles have four, clearly-defined strategies:

(1) planning, design of processes, selection of indicators, deployment of requirements

(2) execution of plans

(3) assessment of progress, taking into account

internal and external indicators

(4) revision of plans, taking into account progress, learning, and new information

7. The Criteria emphasize quality system alignment.

The Criteria call for improvement cycles to occur at all levels and in all parts of the company. In order to ensure that such improvement cycles carried out in different parts of the organization do not operate at counterpurposes, overall aims need to be consistent or aligned. Alignment in the Award Criteria is achieved via interconnecting and mutually reinforcing key indicators, derived from overall company requirements. The latter relate directly to delivery of customer value, improvement of organizational performance, or both. The use of key indicators channels activities toward agreed-upon goals. At the same time, use of indicators avoids detailed procedural prescriptions or unnecessary centralization of process management. Key indicators provide a basis for deploying customer and company performance requirements to all work units. Such alignment ensures consistency while at the same time challenging work units to consider new approaches to superior performance.

Linkage of the Award Criteria to Quality-Related Corporate Issues

Incremental and Breakthrough Improvement

Use of nonprescriptive, results-oriented Criteria and key indicators are intended to focus on what needs to be improved. This approach helps to ensure that improvements throughout the organization contribute to the organization's overall purposes. In addition to supporting creativity in approach and organization, results-oriented Criteria and key indicators encourage "breakthrough thinking"—openness to the possibility for major improvements as well as incremental ones. However, if key indicators are tied too directly to existing work methods, processes, and organizations, breakthrough changes may be discouraged. For this reason, analysis of operations, processes, and progress should focus on the selection of and the value of the indicators themselves. This will help to ensure that indicator selection does not unwittingly contribute to stifling creativity and preventing beneficial changes in organization.

Benchmarks may also serve a useful purpose in stimulating breakthrough thinking. Benchmarks offer the opportunity to achieve significant improvements based on adoption or adaptation of current best practice. In addition, they help encourage creativity through exposure to alternative approaches and results. Also, benchmarks represent a clear challenge to "beat the best," thus encouraging major improvements rather than only incremental refinements of existing approaches. As with key indicators, benchmark selection is critical, and benchmarks should be reviewed periodically for appropriateness.

Financial Performance

The Award Criteria address financial performance via three major avenues: (1) emphasis on quality factors and management actions that lead to better market performance, market share gain, and customer retention; (2) emphasis on improved productivity, asset utilization, and lower overall operating costs; and (3) support for business strategy development and business decisions.

The focus on superior offerings and lower costs of operation means that the Criteria's principal route to improved financial performance is through requirements that seek to channel activities toward producing superior overall value. Delivering superior value—an important part of business strategy—also supports other business strategies such as pricing. For example, superior value offers the possibility of price premiums or competing via lower prices, which may enhance market share and asset utilization, and thus may also contribute to improved financial performance.

Business strategy usually addresses factors in addition to quality and value. For example, strategy may address market niche, facilities location, diversification, acquisition, export development, research, technology leadership, and rapid product turnover. A basic premise of the Award Criteria is that quality principles support the development and evaluation of business decisions and strategies, even though many factors other than product and service quality must be considered. Examples of applications of the Criteria to business decisions and strategies include:

■ quality management of the information used in business decisions and strategy—scope, validity, and analysis

■ quality requirements of niches, new businesses, export target markets

■ quality status of acquisitions—key benchmarks

■ analysis of factors—societal, regulatory, economic, competitive, and risk—that may bear upon the success or failure of strategy

■ development of scenarios built around possible outcomes of strategy or decisions including risks of failures, probable consequences of failures, and management of failure

- lessons learned from previous strategy developments—within the company or available through research.

The Award Criteria and evaluation system take into account market share, customer retention, customer satisfaction, productivity, asset utilization, and other factors that contribute to financial performance. However, the Criteria do not call for aggregate financial information such as quarterly or annual profits in evaluation of applications for Awards. This exclusion is made for several reasons—technical, fairness, and procedural:

- short-term profits may be affected by such factors as accounting practices, business decisions, write-offs, dividends, and investments.

- some industries historically have higher profit levels than others.

- the time interval between quality improvement and overall financial improvement depends upon many factors. Nor would this interval likely be the same from industry to industry or even for companies in the same industry.

- the Award Criteria measure performance relative to rigorous, customer-oriented, company-performance criteria. Though improved quality may improve a company's financial performance, its financial performance depends also on the quality performance of competitors—which the Award process cannot measure directly. The inclusion of aggregate financial indicators in evaluations would place at a disadvantage many applicants in the most competitive businesses.

- financial performance depends upon many external factors, such as local, national, and international economic conditions and business cycles. Such conditions and cycles do not have the same impact on all companies.

- some companies would not participate in the Award process if required to provide more detailed financial information.

Invention, Innovation, and Creativity

Invention, innovation, and creativity—discovery, novel changes to existing practices or products, and imaginative approaches—are important aspects of delivering ever-improving value to customers and maximizing productivity. While state of technology may play a key role in corporate involvement in research leading to discovery, innovation and creativity are crucial features in company competitiveness and can be applied to products, processes, services, human resource development, and overall quality systems.

The Award Criteria encourage invention, innovation, and creativity in all aspects of company decisions and in all work areas:

- nonprescriptive criteria, supported by benchmarks and indicators, encourage creativity and breakthrough thinking as they channel activities toward purpose, not toward following procedures.

- customer-driven quality places major emphasis on the "positive side of quality," which stresses enhancement, new services, and customer relationship management. Success with the positive side of quality depends heavily on creativity—usually more so than steps to reduce errors and defects which tend to rely more on well-defined quality techniques.

- human resource utilization stresses employee involvement, development, and recognition, and encourages creative approaches to improving employee effectiveness, empowerment, and contributions.

- continuous improvement and cycles of learning are integral parts of the activities of all work groups. This requires analysis and problem solving everywhere within the company.

- strong emphasis on cycle time reduction in all company operations encourages companies to analyze work paths, work organization, and the value-added contribution of all process steps, thus fostering change, innovation, and creative thinking in how work is organized and conducted.

- strong emphasis on cycle time and design encourages rapid introduction of new products and services, including those based on new concepts emerging from research areas.

- quality and quality improvement requirements are deployed to all work units, including research, development, and other groups which have responsibility for addressing future requirements. For such groups, measures and indicators are expected to reflect quality, productivity, and effectiveness appropriate to the exploratory nature of their activities.

- focusing on future requirements of customers,

customer segments, and customers of competitors encourages companies to think in terms of attributes and, hence, innovative and creative ways to serve needs.

Changes from the 1991 Award Criteria

The 1992 Award Criteria are built upon the same seven-category framework and use the same approach as in 1991. However, numerous changes have been made to improve clarity and to strengthen key themes. Major changes are:

■ The number of items has been reduced from 32 to 28. A description of the actual changes is summarized, by Category, below.

■ The number of Areas to Address has been reduced from 99 to 89.

■ Point values have been adjusted to provide a better overall balance among items and to place more emphasis on results.

■ An expanded introductory section entitled "Description of the 1992 Award Criteria" replaces the "Description of the 1991 Examination." The purpose of this new section is to enhance the educational value of the Criteria for wider usage—training, self-assessment, and design of quality systems, as well as actual Award applications.

Key Themes Strengthened In the 1992 Criteria

■ cycle time reduction

■ productivity

■ work process and organization simplification and waste reduction

■ relationship between quality and other business management considerations: business planning, financial results, overall company effectiveness, innovation, and future orientation

■ alignment of requirements in plans

■ design quality and prevention

■ data aggregation, analysis, and use

■ work force development

■ quality system integration via Category 6.0

A summary of the most significant changes from 1991,

by Category, follows:

Leadership
■ The Category has been reduced from four to three items. The Quality Values Item (1991) has been subsumed in Items 1.1 and 1.2.

■ The importance of personal involvement of senior executive leadership has been further stressed through increased point value and greater emphasis on executives' personal use of improvement processes.

■ The Management for Quality Item (1992) now requires applicants to analyze their organizational structures to determine how well they support quality, cycle time, and innovation objectives. The intent of this change is to encourage users of the Criteria to work toward organizations capable of speed and flexibility, maximizing value-added work.

Information and Analysis
■ The importance of Item 2.3 has been increased and is now more clearly the "central intelligence" item within the Criteria. This Item serves as the analysis point for the development of company strategy and plans and for the review of company progress. Analyses carried out in Item 2.3 support the dual, results-oriented goals given [in the section Award Criteria Purposes above].

■ The Item addressing Competitive Comparisons and Benchmarks now requires applicants to describe how benchmark data encourage innovation and better knowledge of processes.

Strategic Quality Planning
■ Item 3.1 seeks to provide a better integration of quality and performance planning into overall business planning. Planning issues such as research and development and technology leadership are now more explicitly addressed.

■ Together, Items 3.1 and 3.2 place more emphasis on the process the company uses to deploy customer and company performance requirements to all company units. The importance of such deployment is discussed under quality system alignment [item 7 under the section Key Characteristics of the Award Criteria above].

Human Resource Development and Management
■ The title of this Category has been changed to better reflect development and the investment in human resources which the Category seeks to bal-

ance with utilization.

- More emphasis is placed on improvement of personnel practices such as recruitment and management to achieve excellence, taking into account a more diverse work force.

Management of Process Quality

- The title of this Category has been changed to reflect the greater emphasis on definition, management, and improvement of processes.

- The Category has been reduced from seven to five items. The themes of the 1991 Continuous Improvement of Processes Item have been built into all items of the Category. The 1991 Documentation Item requirements have been included under the Quality Assessment Item for 1992.

- Research and development work of companies with such activities can be described in one or more of three Items: 5.1, 5.2, and 5.3. Product research and development is covered under 5.1; process research is covered under 5.2; and basic research is covered under 5.3. Applicants are not expected to reveal proprietary research and development activities. However, they are expected to provide information on how they use quality principles in managing research and development for greater innovation and better coupling to the company's chosen directions.

Quality and Operational Results

- The title of this Category has been changed to better reflect its dual purposes and the composite nature of results.

- The Category has been increased from three to four Items. The Business Process, Operational, and Support Service Quality Results Item (1991) has been divided into two items to provide better clarity and focus. The four items of this Category are described in detail [in the section The Pivotal Role of the Quality and Operational Results Category above].

Customer Focus and Satisfaction

- The title of this Category has been changed to better reflect its overall purposes.

- The Category has been reduced from eight items to six. Customer Relationship Management (1992) is a composite of three items from the 1991 Criteria: Customer Relationship Management; Customer Service Standards; and Complaint Resolution for Quality Improvement.

- The 1991 Item, Determining Customer Requirements and Expectations, is given more of a future orientation in 1992. The new title of the Item is Future Requirements and Expectations of Customers. This Item (7.6) occurs last in the sequence. The first five Items in the Category are devoted to current and near-term customer issues.

Business Factors Considered in the Evaluation of Applications

The Award Examination is designed to permit evaluation of any quality system for manufacturing and service companies of any size, type of business, or scope of market. The 28 Items and 89 Areas to Address have been selected because of their importance to virtually all businesses. Nevertheless, the importance of the Items and Areas to Address may not be equally applicable to all businesses, even to businesses of comparable size in the same industry. Specific business factors that may bear upon the evaluation are considered at every stage of evaluation. Below is an outline of key business factors considered in the Award Examination.

Key Business Factors

- size and resources of the applicant

- number and types of employees

- nature of the applicant's business: products, services, and technologies used

- special requirements of customers or markets

- scope of the applicant's market: local, regional, national, or international

- regulatory environment within which the applicant operates

- importance of suppliers, dealers, and other external businesses to the applicant and the degree of influence the applicant has over its suppliers

Application Overview

Applicants need to submit a four-page Overview that addresses key business factors that must be considered in the Award evaluation process. The Overview is intended to "set the stage" for the Examiners who conduct the evaluation.

Information that **should be included** in the Overview:

- types of major products and services

- key quality requirements for products and services

- nature of major markets (local, regional, national, or international)

- description of principal customers (consumers, other businesses, government)

- competitive environment

- applicant's position in the industry

- major equipment and facilities used

- types of technologies used

- general description of the applicant's employee base, including: number, type, and educational level

- importance of and types of suppliers of goods and services

- occupational health and safety, environmental, and other regulatory considerations

- other factors important to the applicant

If the applicant of a subsidiary, a description of the organizational structure and management links to the parent company should be presented. Subsidiaries should also include information that shows key relationships to the parent company: (1) percent of employees; (2) percent of sales; and (3) types of products and services. (The overview is not counted as part of the page limit.)

1992 EXAMINATION ITEMS AND POINT VALUES

1992 Examination Categories/Items	Point Values

1.0 Leadership — 90

1.1	Senior Executive Leadership	45
1.2	Management for Quality	25
1.3	Public Responsibility	20

2.0 Information and Analysis — 80

2.1	Scope and Management of Quality and Performance Data and Information	15
2.2	Competitive Comparisons and Benchmarks	25
2.3	Analysis and Uses of Company-Level Data	40

3.0 Strategic Quality Planning — 60

3.1	Strategic Quality and Company Performance Planning Process	35
3.2	Quality and Performance Plans	25

4.0 Human Resource Development and Management — 150

4.1	Human Resource Management	20
4.2	Employee Involvement	40
4.3	Employee Education and Training	40
4.4	Employee Performance and Recognition	25
4.5	Employee Well-Being and Morale	25

5.0 Management of Process Quality — 140

5.1	Design and Introduction of Quality Products and Services	40
5.2	Process Management—Product and Service Production and Delivery Processes	35
5.3	Process Management—Business Processes and Support Services	30
5.4	Supplier Quality	20
5.5	Quality Assessment	15

6.0 Quality and Operational Results — 180

6.1	Product and Service Quality Results	75
6.2	Company Operational Results	45

6.3	Business Process and Support Service Results	25
6.4	Supplier Quality Results	35
7.0	**Customer Focus and Satisfaction**	**300**
7.1	Customer Relationship Management	65
7.2	Commitment to Customers	15
7.3	Customer Satisfaction Determination	35
7.4	Customer Satisfaction Results	75
7.5	Customer Satisfaction Comparison	75
7.6	Future Requirements and Expectations of Customers	35
TOTAL POINTS		**1,000**

Figure 1-3: Examination Items and Point Values

Chapter Two

Malcolm Baldrige National Quality Award Winners—1988

Globe Metallurgical Inc.

By talking with customers, finding out exactly what they expect in terms of products and services, and incorporating their suggestions and teachings into its quality process, this company achieved excellence—and easily earned the first Baldrige Award for a small business.

Globe Metallurgical Inc. (Beverly, OH)—a 210-employee producer of metal and ferrosilicon products—can be noted for three significant factors regarding its winning the Malcolm Baldrige National Quality Award in 1988:

❶ *It won the first year the Award was offered.*
❷ *It was the first small business to win the Award.*
❸ *One vice president sat down and wrote Globe's Award winning application in one weekend.*

In addition to these items, another point that makes Globe's winning the Baldrige Award noteworthy is that the facility is really not what might come to mind when one envisions the ultimate high-quality workplace. When most people think of quality, they tend to picture clean, neat, sparkling, high-tech workplaces. But Globe far from fits that ideal.

"We are probably one of the 'heaviest' industries to ever be involved in the Baldrige process," concedes Curtis W. Goins, director of Quality and Research and Development. "By that, I mean we don't have a nice, wonderful, clean place to work in: We have an open, unheated, smoky, hot place because we handle molten metals, which generate a lot of smoke and sparks. Globe is not a pristine electronic corporation, or a Xerox, or a company like that. It's very much a 'smokestack' business."

Yet another interesting fact about Globe's winning the Baldrige Award is that the company became aware of the Award only about *two weeks* before they applied for it, Goins recalls. "That was the first year the Award was offered. Baldrige representatives were at a booth passing out applications at a Quality Conference we attended. We reviewed the application very quickly and decided to apply."

SIMPLY "TELLING IT LIKE IT IS" BRINGS BALDRIGE SURPRISE

The information for Globe's application was initially gathered by four people at the Beverly, Ohio plant: the vice president of Human Resources, the plant manager, the quality manager, and Goins. They divided up the seven sections of the application according to what they thought each person could best handle.

> **"If management is <u>persistent</u> and <u>consistent</u>, particularly persistent—and exhibits real dedication to the process in a way that makes employees <u>see</u>, <u>feel</u>, and <u>know</u> their commitment is true—then employees begin to come on board almost in a landslide."**

Award Winning Quality

(Each of the four actually contributed to several sections.) All the information they gathered was then given to the vice president of Quality and Administration, who sat down at his computer and wrote the complete application over one weekend.

"We won the first time we submitted an application, so naturally, we were very pleased with our results," Goins reports. "However, we did not *expect* to win—we simply wanted to use the Baldrige application as another means of improving ourselves."

Although it came easily, there was no trick to Globe's win: The company simply stated the quality facts as they were. "We just told about the systems we had established over the last two to three years," Goins explains. "We were able to give examples of what we had done to address various questions because the Baldrige criteria were very similar to the criteria that our customers had in their quality systems.

"We had also made great strides in productivity improvement," he continues. "Many of the sections in the Baldrige application recognized improvements in productivity as part of the total management system. Our systems were already in place—the Baldrige people simply recognized that they were superior, and recognized us with the Award.

"For Globe, it was not a matter of *get the Baldrige and then develop a system*. It was a matter of *develop a system, and then apply for the Baldrige*," Goins stresses.

Indeed, Globe had managed to easily skate through

a process that often befuddles other organizations. Many companies that seek to apply for the Baldrige Award are completely confused by the complexity of the questions and the requests for data to support their statements. How did Globe seem to so easily cut through this process with one sweep of the blade?

■ **First,** the firm already had a well-established quality process in place that met the Baldrige criteria.

■ **Second,** this process was very well documented, so Globe was able to readily provide the statistical data and other information necessary to win the Award.

What steps did Globe follow to arrive at such an effective quality process? A detailed look at its strategy is provided below.

THE DEVELOPMENT OF A FIRST-RATE QUALITY PROCESS

Globe had long been well established in the domestic ferroalloy marketplace, but in the mid-1980s, quality became even more important to the way the company provided and marketed its products. This occurred for two reasons:

➤ *Customers started emphasizing quality.*
➤ *International competition was on the rise.*

To survive in an industry where companies were being forced out of business, Globe had to go the extra mile to prove its capabilities. The company shifted its focus from commodity markets, such as steel manufacturing, to higher value-added markets, such as foundries. It also started a quality program that involved customers, employees, and suppliers in its effort.

"We concentrated on improving the quality of products and processes, and lowering the cost of producing the alloys that we do best," Goins explains. "It would be meaningless to have the best quality in the world if it was so expensive that no one could afford it. By the same turn, if we had the lowest price in the world but no one wanted the product because of poor quality, we'd be missing the mark."

Here are the steps Globe took to develop the process that helped it to assure both cost- and quality-effectiveness:

★ **Learn from customers.** Some of Globe's larger customers, primarily auto makers, had started focusing on consolidating their supplier bases by doing business only with suppliers that were able to meet their stringent specifications and deliver top-quality materials.

To make sure they chose the best of the best, some customers had begun providing suppliers such as Globe with stringent specifications, and auditing these suppliers' quality systems.

To become a recognized quality supplier, Globe turned to its customers for help, studying their requirements for awards and/or certifications. "We worked with our customers to develop an improved quality system, and we took advantage of all the insight that they could give us," Goins says. "These customers were such companies as Ford Motor Company, General Motors Corporation, and several iron, steel, and chemical companies. They helped us by auditing our quality system and providing information about how to develop a 'world class' quality process."

For example, to make its quality expectations abundantly clear to its suppliers, Ford issued a document called Q-101, which is a manual of quality specs. Ford also established the American Supplier Institute to train suppliers in specific methods to improve quality. In addition, Ford offered exceptional suppliers a Q-1 Award, while General Motors offered its suppliers a SPEAR certification.

"We also took some courses ourselves to find out how to create and manage a quality system," Goins adds. "We went through the Q-1 process with Ford, and we learned a great deal about quality systems and statistical quality control."

★ **Provide quality training.** Quality training at Globe includes these two components:

● *Employee training.* When Globe realized that its entire work force had to be trained in at least the fundamentals of SPC, they had Ford's American Supplier Institute send a trainer to Beverly to train in-house. Following this, a Globe quality team trained the Selma, Alabama, division employees themselves. After that, their quality manager developed their programs.

● *Supplier training.* "Suppliers that want to improve quality and lower costs are the only ones we want to talk to," Goins asserts. Globe wants its suppliers to respond to its needs as effectively as Globe responds to its own customers' needs. So the company shows its suppliers the improvements it has made in response to customer suggestions, and teaches them how to implement SPC so that they can better control *their own* products.

This supplier involvement effort started after Globe trained all its own employees in quality methods. The company invited five major suppliers in and trained them in the fundamentals of quality and SPC. Then they visited other major suppliers and trained *their* employees in SPC. The Globe trainers left training materials, blank charts, and even calculators at each supplier's site so that the suppliers could continue training *their own* employees.

Suppliers are asked to furnish the same types of control charts that Globe uses internally to check its own processes. These charts must be provided on all critical parameters, and they must indicate whether the product is consistent, what variations occurred during processing, and other pertinent information.

(To add another link to the supplier quality chain, Globe also asks its suppliers to audit *their* suppliers, which further improves consistency and lowers costs, Goins notes.)

"As a result of these efforts, our suppliers' quality systems mirror Globe's quite closely, and the charts they provide match the parameters the QEC Committee expects," Goins reports. "The same processes that improve product quality and consistency also lower costs, so it's a win-win situation," he adds.

When suppliers deliver more consistent materials, Globe saves money in two ways:

➤ There are fewer process upsets due to fluctuations in materials, so more product can be manufactured using the same amount of raw materials.

➤ When suppliers save money, those savings are passed on to customers. "Suppliers get a larger share of our business as their product improves and their costs go down," says Goins. "Eventually, we may target one to be a certified supplier and maybe even a single-source supplier."

★ **Implement statistical process control (SPC).** Goins explains that SPC is a means for plotting data to determine whether processes are operating within specified quality parameters. For example, suppose employees need to check the length of some metal bars that must be four feet long. Plotting the lengths of the bars as they are being manufactured enables employees to

⊃ Determine the average length of the bars being produced and how much the length varies during the process. This then allows workers to spot and correct defect trends *before* the bars actually fall out of spec.

⊃ Monitor the range between the longest and shortest bars so that employees can narrow this range and keep it under control.

"You can use SPC procedures with any type of measurement, whether it's a percentage, rate of return, or other measurement," asserts Goins. "The real challenge is to identify the right variables to manage, and then learn what to do when a process starts to show a trend toward going out of spec. You need to determine what to correct and what not to correct.

And that's all covered by statistical process control training."

Supervisors at Globe were given SPC training, and later, hourly workers were trained as well. Also, the American Supplier Institute customized a general SPC program specifically for Globe. "We wanted to talk about pouring temperatures, percent silicon, and other matters that were important to Globe," explains Goins. "We asked trainers to help our people to prepare real charts with real data so that after they completed their training, they could take those charts and continue to use them on the floor."

With SPC charting, management can track process quality. "Part of statistical process control is being able to calculate process capability," says Goins. "In other words, you can determine how well the process meets the needs of the customer. If you track the process capability from month to month, you can see improvements in the ability of that particular process to meet either internal or external customer needs." Current output, including statistical goals for product parameters and control variables (see below), are posted daily for all employees to see.

★ **Conduct quality systems audits.** Globe had always been regarded as a producer of the highest quality alloys in the industry. Chemical laboratories at both of Globe's plants had state-of-the-art analytical equipment, and all products were carefully scrutinized before shipment. This 100-percent inspection proved costly but effective.

When the auto giants started offering quality audits, Globe asked Ford to audit its quality systems. Globe scored 139 points out of a possible 200, only one point short of the 140 needed to pass. With the need to install even more sophisticated quality systems, Globe formed an in-house team to assess customer audits.

The team was initially composed of the quality manager, staff metallurgist, and vice president of Human Resources. It was called the Quality, Efficiency, and Cost (QEC) committee. Later, it became known as the QEC Steering Committee, and all top company officials became members. Soon afterward, QEC Committees composed of the plant managers and department heads were formed at each plant. These Committees examine their plants' SPC results daily, and meet with individuals or teams in problem areas to discuss what resources they need to do a quality job.

★ **Utilize audit information to develop effective, company-specific quality tools.** After conducting its initial in-house audits, the original QEC team identified five key "tools" that would become essential parts of Globe's quality system. These elements were

❶ *Procedures.* These include exactly what steps are

involved in making a particular product, and how employees in different functions interact to make that product.

❷ **Job Work Instructions (JWIs).** These are similar to procedures but are much narrower in scope. They include specific instructions on how each individual controls the process to generate a consistent product, and what parameters to measure for a consistent product.

❸ **Critical Process Variables (CPVs).** These are the variables that must be controlled within the system to assure that the final product is within parameters.

❹ **Product Parameters (PPs).** These are the parameters the customer is particularly interested in controlling. They involve SPC charting and process capability assessment.

❺ **Failure Mode Effects Analysis (FMEAs).** These involve assessing such matters as what causes a parameter to go out of control? What is the probability that the company will detect the problem before the customer does? FMEAs can be used in the following ways:

➤ **First,** they enable management to prioritize activities according to what products have the highest probability of reaching a customer with defects.

➤ **Second,** they can be a source of information when posted with SPC charts. "What might go out of control and how it might be corrected can be gleaned from FMEAs and posted as a list of factors to check when a process is out of control," Goins explains.

★ **Enlist top management leadership.** "To get total employee involvement, you must first have *leadership* in your company—the very top corporate management must be committed to the quality process," Goins stresses.

"You must also have top corporate management explain to workers that if they expect to keep their jobs and to keep the company open and running, they are going to have to make some rather dramatic changes in the way they do things. Employees needed to understand that we *had* to improve the quality of our products and our systems to ensure top quality, as well as to improve the way the company is run.

"As we found out, if management is *persistent* and *consistent,* particularly persistent—and exhibits real dedication to the process in a way that makes employees *see, feel,* and *know* their commitment is true— then employees begin to come on board almost in a

landslide," Goins continues. "When this starts, the leaders in the hourly work force are the ones to say that the workers have to do this or that to improve. Pretty soon, *everyone* becomes part of the process and makes suggestions on ways to improve."

★ **Involve and recognize employees.** One way Globe keeps its employees involved and motivated is with *empowerment*. "We let employees know that the success or failure of the business or of the product group they are involved with depends upon the quality of the product they produce and the decisions they make," says Goins.

"We train employees to handle the responsibility of decision-making, and we give them the tools and support they need. Every success they have in problem-solving or in product improvement generates pride and ownership."

Employees at Globe serve on problem-solving teams that started out as quality circles, and have since become more product oriented, instead of process oriented. A team may be composed of employees who would otherwise not be exposed to an entire process— from purchasing raw materials to shipping finished products.

The teams examine the technology behind products, the products' characteristics, and other key factors. They may also investigate causes of product failure by learning how products are used and by tracing the manufacture of products from suppliers in the plant, to their internal customers, and then out to external customers.

Recognition plays a large role in Globe's employee participation effort, and takes several forms:

➤ **Visits to customer sites.** Individual workers and teams who contribute particularly noteworthy ideas are recognized by being invited to travel to customers' facilities. There, the employees get a real quality learning experience under their belts: They have the opportunity to talk to the customers' employees and find out how Globe's products are used, what the customers' employees consider important about the products, and what, if anything, they might like to see changed about the products.

"Our employees may think that the products themselves are what's important, but it may actually be the *packaging* that's a problem to the customers," notes Goins. "The customers' employees who do the handling may never complain to anyone else, but they'll tell our hourly employees about the problem."

During these visits, Globe employees also learn how their products contribute to society and how product failure can result in tragedy. "For instance, workers learn that the failure of a part made with poor product may lead to a car crash," says Goins. "And they don't want to be responsible for that type of failure."

➤ **Letters of recognition.** Workers who contribute suggestions for improvement are also given personal recognition in the form of letters from the company president, which are mailed to their homes so that the employees' families can participate in the reward, too.

➤ **Gifts.** Other forms of recognition are jackets, hats, and other gifts, which are awarded for team as well as for individual efforts.

PRIZES ACCRUE AS QUALITY IMPROVEMENTS CONTINUE

Since implementing its comprehensive quality program, Globe has made extensive headway in penetrating international markets. It has also made significant internal improvements concerning efficiency, products returned for replacement, customer complaints, employee accidents, and absenteeism.

Goins attributes the success of Globe's quality efforts to two key factors: employee enthusiasm and customer satisfaction. "Had it not been for our customers' urging, instruction, patience, and guidance, I don't think we could have done it," he says, "It would have been much more difficult."

The efforts to improve continue onward. "We certainly didn't stop our quality improvement efforts with the Malcolm Baldrige [application process]," Goins adds. "We have continued to improve our system. We now call it the 'Total Management System,' rather than just the 'Quality System.' This new system has been recognized with the first-ever Shingo Prize for manufacturing excellence, administered out of the University of Utah. We won the Shingo the year after we won the Baldrige."

> **"We listen, we learn, and we act constantly so that the quality of our products and services will keep improving."**

"We are also one of fewer than 20 suppliers worldwide to receive Ford's 'Total Quality Excellence Award,' which requires that you have a Total Quality Management system in place," he continues. "In addition, we've received General Motors' 'Targets for Excellence,' which is another total quality management system review.

"More recently, in 1991 our European division received ISO (International Standards Organization) 9000 certification. We have become the only certified supplier to Saturn Motors Corporation in the world.

"So we have continued to advance our quality systems," Goins stresses. "We continue to seek internal and external advice on how to correct deficiencies. We *listen,* we *learn,* and we *act* constantly so that the quality of our products and services will keep improving."

A Master Calendar Helps Keep a Master Quality Plan on Track

To keep an award winning quality plan on track, you need an effective, yet nonthreatening way to remind all company managers about deadlines, milestones, appointments, and other significant dates and events. To that end, Globe Metallurgical Inc. uses a "master calendar" as a critical planning tool in conjunction with its five-year strategy for improving quality and cutting costs.

According to Curtis W. Goins, director of Quality and Research and Development, this calendar keeps the company's 30 managers informed and helps them organize their time. "Everyone in the company has different functions to perform," he says. "There are audits, evaluations, benchmarks, and agendas, and they have to be done by certain dates.

"The calendar is a resource-planning tool. We use it as a reminder so that everyone knows what everyone else is working on, what the deadlines are, and to whom to go for help, etc. This draws us all a little closer together."

MAKING THEIR MARKS

"People always mark appointments and things they have to do on a calendar," Goins explains. "So we just extended this idea for our managers and mark things for them." Keeping everyone on track is important at Globe, where the company's five-year plan consists of a 20-page list containing more than 100 items. With so many projects, the master calendar lets managers know what they must accomplish in the coming year.

The calendar is produced by computer software and consists of a page for each month. A Quality, Efficiency, and Cost Committee develops a proposed calendar that managers review and amend as needed. Once managers approve the calendar, entries are filled in, and each manager is given a completed calendar. Entries may be added later as additional appointments or other activities are scheduled.

The blocks for each day contain shorthand references to items on the five-year plan. One day's entry might read: *#56—Curt Goins, visit Union Carbide Corp., perform supplier quality audit.* Managers can then refer to the numbered plan for more details and deadlines.

"We try to plan activities in advance and prevent conflicts on the calendar," Goins says. "We don't want to send too many of our salaried people away from the plant at any given time. We also don't want to overload them with too many things to do.

"At the same time, the calendar is also a management tool for assigning responsibility and completion dates." However, its purpose is not simply to make managers accountable, but to constantly remind them of what steps to take to meet deadlines. "The calendar prods them," Goins notes. "They look at their calendars every day. They know what they have to do and to whom they have to talk. They can flip the page and see what's coming up the next month and organize their time so that they can get activities scheduled in advance and not wait until the last minute."

GET FULL AGREEMENT FROM EVERYONE INVOLVED

Goins advises companies interested in using a calendar to *be sure that managers agree to what is scheduled* before it is finalized and distributed. He also notes that you don't need any tools to devise your own calendar. "You can use any tool you want; you don't need software," he says. "You can take a piece of paper and a pencil and draw up a calendar. What's more important is *to have an effective plan that is dedicated to continuous quality improvement.*" That's what Globe has, and it's got an Award to prove it.

Motorola, Inc.

Six Sigma Performance and Quality Systems Review teams helped this winning company to set zero-defects performance goals, train employees in how to meet those goals, and then keep its quality process on track so that it could move ever onward toward success.

Although Motorola, Inc. (Schaumburg, IL), had always had quality initiatives in place, the Baldrige-winning company realized that it needed to become even *more* aggressive in the area of world-class quality. Recognizing that "quality is in the eye of the customer," one area that Motorola chose to place special emphasis on was customer satisfaction.

"Previously, most of our quality efforts had dealt exclusively with product quality," reports Carlton Braun, vice president and director of the Motorola Management Institute. However, other areas besides poor product quality can have a negative impact on customer satisfaction. For example, if we have a problem with our billing process that takes two or three months to straighten out, the customer is not going to be satisfied, even if the product works perfectly."

With this type of situation in mind, Motorola set a goal to instill its Total Customer Satisfaction (TCS) philosophy throughout the organization. To do that requires breaking down "silos."

> **"In almost all cases, employees _want_ to do a good job, so it is important to give them the tools to perform their jobs properly."**

According to Braun, silos are conceptual representations of what might be termed "departmental isolation." Most companies tend to operate under this silo concept, in which employees in each department are interested only in "polishing silo walls" (that is, making sure they work for the good of their own departments rather than for the good of the whole company).

Motorola's goal was to break down these silos and get employees to realize the importance of seeing the larger picture—and ultimately performing their jobs with the *whole process* in mind. "We wanted our people to cooperate with one another for support of total

customer satisfaction," Braun explains.

IDENTIFYING SYSTEM WEAKNESSES BREAKS DOWN BARRIERS

Part of breaking down barriers involves addressing the "system" weaknesses that lead to so many problems. In most organizations, as has been demonstrated time and again, 20 percent of errors are caused by employees themselves (factors within their own control), while the other 80 percent are caused by the problems within the systems in which the employees work (issues for which *management* has responsibility).

In production, for example, problems beyond an operator's control might include such factors as the following:

➤ *poorly designed assemblies*

➤ *incorrect parts being ordered or shipped by suppliers*

➤ *defective or damaged parts from suppliers*

➤ *machinery incapable of operating within control limits*

➤ *insufficient training*

"In almost all cases, employees *want* to do a good job, so it is important to give them the tools to perform their jobs properly," Braun asserts.

THE SIX SIGMA SOLUTION SETS TIGHT PERFORMANCE PARAMETERS

One step Motorola has taken to address the issue of customer satisfaction is "Six Sigma Performance." Six Sigma Performance is a level of variation in a process measured in standard deviations from the mean and is defined as 99.9997 percent defect-free, or 3.4 defects per million parts produced. (See Figure 2-1 near the end of this section.)

While many companies limit their process improvement efforts to monitoring production control charts, Six Sigma Performance, again, extends beyond production quality. "It addresses variation in performance of *all* kinds," emphasizes Braun. Not only that, but it also addresses performance in all areas of the company, including Order Entry, Sales, Purchasing, Manufacturing, Engineering/Design, Quality Control, and so on.

IT STARTS WITH COMPREHENSIVE EMPLOYEE TRAINING

To kick off the process, the company's training department developed a step-by-step process designed to promote understanding and implementation of Six Sigma Performance throughout the entire organization. All employees going through the training learn the concepts and tools that help them reduce variation in the work they perform.

The first module of training takes one to three days to complete, depending on the level of the employees in the organization who are taking the training. After training, employees work in teams in their departments and across functions to utilize what they have learned, which should include the following:

➡ *To understand the system in which they are working* by mapping the system step-by-step.

➡ *To look for places where variations/errors occur.* In many cases, simply mapping the work process itself helps employees to spot these variations.

➡ *To determine the cause of the problems.* This may include lack of proper tools, improper training, or an incorrect system, to name a few.

➡ *To reduce the cycle time of a process as much as possible.* "If you have a lengthy cycle time, you have more chance for errors than if you have a short cycle time," Braun notes. A reduction in cycle time, then, leads to an improvement in quality.

Training employees in the use of this procedure is one thing; making sure they use it on a regular basis—instead of reverting to "Band-Aid" solutions—is quite another. Motorola addresses this issue in two ways:

■ **Providing additional training opportunities for employees.** Employees have the opportunity to attend additional training programs covering statistical process control (SPC), design for manufacturing, design for assembly, short-cycle-time manufacturing, JIT, and other areas. "These programs help support Six Sigma Performance initiatives," explains Braun.

■ **Manager training in coaching skills.** Managers receive training in the importance of coaching their employees. "It's easy for managers to get caught up in the day-to-day activities of their work and forget the importance of coaching employees in reducing variation," he says. "But when you find a manager who is committed to coaching employees in these procedures, you find employees who are ready, willing, and able to use the procedures," Braun notes.

REVIEWS KEEP THE SYSTEM GOING STRONG

A company can have the best quality system in the world. But if it fails to keep the process on course, its quality effort is doomed to failure. To keep *its* process on track, Motorola established a highly effective review system.

"One of the provisions of the award was that, in winning, a company share its nonproprietary systems with other companies," says Scott Shumway, vice president and director of Quality for Motorola's Semiconductor Sector (Phoenix, AZ). "We've done that with a series of presentations to customers and suppliers; we're always happy to tell what works for us."

> **"We've developed the system to the point that we can see at a glance trends against goals, cost of nonconformance, quality of delivery, service to customers, and so on, complete with a summary."**

"Motorola's quality progress started when we saw a need for much more intensive training in quality at all levels," Shumway explains. "This led to formation of our Motorola Corporate Quality Council, or MCQC, which directs quality efforts throughout the company." The Quality Systems Review is one significant tool that helped Motorola advance its zero-defect, Total Customer Satisfaction philosophy and receive one of the first Baldrige Awards in 1988.

QUALITY TEAMS CONDUCT THE SYSTEMS REVIEWS

Motorola's Quality Systems Review is an internal audit program in which teams of five people from the MCQC visit divisions and spend a week talking with people there and measuring operations against stated criteria.

The teams look at 10 sections or factors that Shumway says are remarkably similar to the points looked at by the administrators who bestow the Malcolm Baldrige Award.

Motorola's basic 10 factors (with assigned weights) are the following:

❶ Quality system management (15 percent). "Here, we look at the leadership, style, and effectiveness of the management team in the area of quality," Shumway explains.

❷ Product development control (10 percent). This area is based on the Six Sigma process. As explained above, Sigma is a statistical unit of measurement that describes the distribution about the mean of a process or procedure. "A process or procedure that can achieve plus or minus Six Sigma capability can be expected to have a defect rate of no more than a few parts per million," Shumway says.

"In statistical terms, this approaches zero defects—and it's our goal to achieve this level of quality in *everything* we do."

❸ Purchasing material control (10 percent). This looks at the level of quality being supplied by vendors and the systems in place to measure vendor quality.

❹ Process development and operational controls (10 percent). "This is aimed at the entire manufacturing flow process," says Shumway. "The critical question is, 'Is it working?'"

❺ Quality data programs (5 percent). Are all necessary data available? Is this real information and not just databases? How is the information used—as a tool to improve quality?

❻ Special studies (10 percent). How sophisticated are the process methods? Are they state-of-the-art?

❼ Quality measurement and control equipment (5 percent). "This governs all our standards and calibrations," says Shumway. "Is the system in place and is it properly maintained?"

❽ Human resources involvement (5 percent). "The team tries to determine whether the people are capable and properly trained," says Shumway. "We want to know if the work force can do the job assigned."

This area is particularly important to Motorola, Shumway explains, because it's a recognized national leader in the participative management process, with people down the ranks involved in decision-making—and sharing in the rewards of correct decisions.

❾ Customer satisfaction assessment (20 percent). All organizations must have methods and systems in place to assess customers' satisfaction with their shipments.

❿ Software quality assurance (10 percent).

"This was a later addition to our list," notes Shumway. "We're getting more and more sophisticated in software related to quality. We spent several years getting people prepared in this area before we tailored it into a score. We've developed the system to the point that we can see at a glance trends against goals, cost of nonconformance, quality of delivery, service to customers, and so on, complete with a summary."

Putting it all together, the division being examined knows how it is doing. "If its score is below the satisfactory mark, the division knows that it needs corrective action," he says.

REVIEW TEAM MEMBERS SELECTED ON A ROTATING BASIS

Motorola's divisions can expect a Quality Service Review every two years. The corporate council puts together a special team for each review, and the five members are selected from various parts of the company. There's no one committee that does all the checking, Shumway notes.

> "Our system has worked well for us. Over the years, it gives us uniformity and consistency. Corporate goals are driven down through the organization, and that's a powerful quality tool."

"We thought about having one fixed team do all the reviews, but decided against it," he explains. "It's better to have people rotated so that every quality director gets an opportunity to work on a team. We also are careful about selecting leaders of each team. No one can be the leader without having participated in Quality Service Reviews in the past.

"At the end of the week of review, the general manager and his or her staff have a session with the team. They go over the review. The strengths and weaknesses are discussed, and recommendations are given to local management as to what improvements have to be made," he says.

Results of the survey are reported to the steering committee, the MCQC, at the next meeting. Results *continued on page 42*

continued on page 42

The variation of any process is measured in Standard Deviations or in Sigmas from the mean, which is the center of the distribution. The normal distribution of a process is considered to be between ±3 Sigmas about the center.

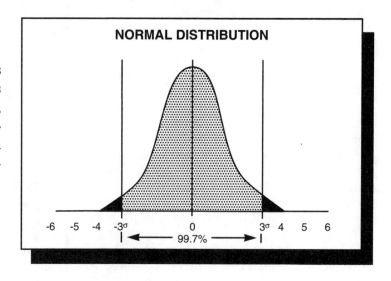

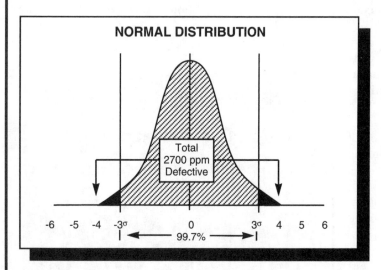

Approximately 2,700 parts per million parts manufactured will fall outside this normal ±3 Sigma variation. This, by itself, does not appear to be disconcerting at first glance.

After all, there are still 997,300 parts within the ±3 Sigma limits. However, when we build a product containing 1,200 parts, or having 1,200 steps, we can expect that the compounding of the out-of-tolerance or defective parts will result in a whopping 3.24 defects per unit on the average; some will have zero, and some will have a lot more. This is a cumulative yield throughout the process of only 4%. This means that only 40 units out of every 1,000 started would go through the entire manufacturing process without a defect.

Thus, we can see that for a product to be built virtually defect-free, it must be designed to accept characteristics that are significantly more than ±3 Sigma away from the mean.

Figure 2-1: Motorola's Six Sigma Performance Process

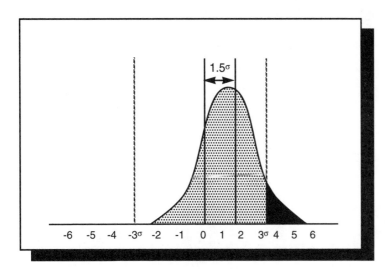

Of course, in real life to compound the problem, the normal distribution curve is unfortunately not always exactly centered and the distribution of parts, or processes, shifts to the right or left. Thus, every time a portion of the normal distribution shifts further past the upper or lower level of an acceptable design, we cause additional defects to occur. These defects must now be found and repaired.

It can be shown that a design that can accept *twice the normal variation* of the process, or ±6 Sigma, can be expected to have no more than 3.4 parts per million defective for each characteristic, instead of 2,700, even if the normal distribution curve were to shift by as much as ±1.5 Sigma off center.

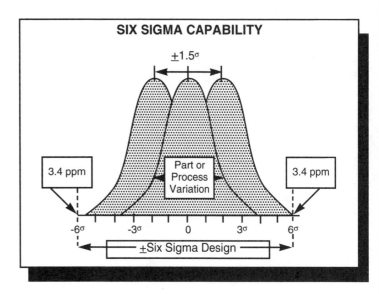

Now, returning to the product containing 1,200 parts or steps, if it is designed for ±6 Sigma capability, instead of ±3 Sigma, we can expect only 0.0041 defects per unit, instead of 3.24. This means that 996 units out of 1,000 would go through the entire manufacturing process without a defect, instead of only 40 out of 1,000.

Our goal is to design products that will accept reasonable variation in component parts, and to develop manufacturing processes that will produce minimum variation in the final output product. *This goal is SIX SIGMA, our 1992 objective.*

Courtesy: Motorola, Inc.

continued from page 39
aren't negotiable; what the team sees is what is reported. At the MCQC meeting, the division manager of the review division reports on what corrective action his or her organization will be taking.

CORPORATE CHAMPIONSHIP CREATES QUALITY CHAMPS

"The Quality Service Review is championed by the corporation," Shumway reports. "That's a key point that we've made to other corporations as we've shared our experiences under the provisions of the Malcolm Baldrige Award.

"Of course, there are some considerations that are proprietary," he concedes. "But for the most part, we're open as to what we do and how it works.

"Our system has worked well for us," Shumway continues. "Over the years, it gives us uniformity and consistency. Corporate goals are driven down through the organization, and that's a powerful quality tool," he concludes.

Westinghouse Electric Corporation

Twelve Conditions of Excellence enabled this division of Westinghouse to create a Total Quality culture throughout its organization—and merit one of the first Baldrige Awards ever given.

To be effective, a total quality process must pervade all levels of the company. First, top management's support is needed to implement new ideas and ultimately to assure the success of the program. Next, careful planning is needed to ensure that all departments and groups work together toward the same goal.

Other essential ingredients include getting all employees involved in making improvements, as well as recognizing them for their efforts. And last but not least, getting customers involved is also crucial so that the organization can offer them exactly what they expect in terms of products and services.

In 1980, Westinghouse Electric Corporation started a companywide quality effort based on the above concepts of Total Quality Management (TQM). This process was implemented as a means to combat the growing threat of competition, and has since evolved into a powerful management model. About the same time the program was implemented, the company also opened a Productivity and Quality Center to develop quality improvement techniques and to spread the message about total quality throughout the entire organization.

Over the years, the Total Quality program has resulted in significant improvements throughout Westinghouse. These efforts were validated when the Commercial Nuclear Fuel Division, or CNFD (Pittsburgh, PA), won one of the first Baldrige Awards in 1988. (This division is composed of a headquarters and three plants, at which a total of 2,200 workers are employed.)

DO IT RIGHT THE FIRST TIME: A TOTAL QUALITY ESSENTIAL

According to the definition that Westinghouse adopted in 1984, Total Quality is "performance leadership in meeting customer requirements by doing the right things right the first time."

To meet this stringent standard, Westinghouse created a culture in which employees at all levels are totally focused on quality. "At CNFD, we've developed a culture where employees involved in quality are the norm," explains Michele M. DeWitt, CNFD's manager for Total Quality. "The Total Quality attitude is so pervasive that it's those who *don't* participate who are the exception," she points out.

Here's how Westinghouse created this quality culture to achieve total quality and become one of the first winners of the Baldrige Award.

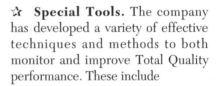

Total Quality is "performance leadership in meeting customer requirements by doing the right things right the first time."

THE ELEMENTS OF A STRONG TOTAL QUALITY PROCESS

Westinghouse incorporates the following factors into its Total Quality process:

Award Winning Quality

☆ **Special Tools.** The company has developed a variety of effective techniques and methods to both monitor and improve Total Quality performance. These include

➤ *Cost/Time Profiles.* These profiles are graphic representations of the buildup of cost over time as a product or service passes through its entire processing cycle. The profiles can be applied to all aspects of the business, and are used for pinpointing specific areas for improvement and quantifying improvement efforts.

➤ *Value-Edge Process.* This computer-aided process focuses on customers' needs by documenting value structures, customers' perceptions of competitors' performance, and relevant value-to-price and value-to-cost ratios. This enables Westinghouse to determine whether processes should be changed to better satisfy customer needs.

☆ **Extensive planning.** At CNFD, a Quality Council coordinates all quality activities within the Division and establishes annual Quality Plan objectives for the Division. Membership in the Quality Council has evolved over the years; the Council is currently composed of the general manager, his staff, and the quality assurance manager at each facility within the Division.

Each Quality Plan has a theme such as "ownership," which was the theme of the company's 1991 plan. Recent plans have followed this format:

○ *A report of the Division's performance during the previous year.* This includes reports from the headquarter's staff and plant managers.

○ *Improvement initiatives or objectives planned for the coming year,* which will be monitored at the division level. Because the plan covers the entire Division, different objectives may apply to different facilities. Objectives are grouped according to the four quality imperatives described above. Each objective is also assigned to a particular person who is held accountable for it, as well as to other specific individuals who serve in support functions.

"We have someone with key accountability so that we know who to approach and say, 'Has this been achieved or hasn't it?'" DeWitt says. "We also identify support from other people throughout other parts of the organization."

A commitment is also made to complete all items by the end of the year. Those that are not completed are carried over to the following year and are sometimes redefined because of changes that occur at the company.

"We're in a dynamic environment where things always change," notes DeWitt. "We also like to stretch ourselves. We don't want plans that are so easy that maybe people could have done more. We try to give them more than they think they might comfortably be able to do that year."

☆ **Employee participation.** The Division may have as many as 310 quality teams at a time working on various projects. Teams have formed and disbanded, and new teams have formed over the years and now include increased participation by nonexempt employees. Various types of teams include

⇨ *Customer teams.* Each of these teams serves a particular customer. A project engineer serves as team leader and is the key person for communicating with that customer. Teams may be composed of the project engineer and several individuals from Engineering, Manufacturing, and Quality Assurance.

"We're very close to our customers," says DeWitt. "Our project engineers and engineers on customer teams speak daily with their counterparts in the cus-

tomers' organizations about analyses that are being done or products that are being built. Our customers place long-term, large-dollar-amount contracts, and each customer is very different. We have evolved into a contract-specific custom builder."

⇨ *Conditions of excellence teams.* One of these teams is formed at each site within the Division and is responsible for developing ideas for the annual quality plan. There is a lead employee for each of the 12 Conditions of Excellence (see below).

These teams identify strengths and weaknesses, pinpoint areas for improvement, develop ideas on how to make improvements, and so on. That pool of ideas is then submitted to the Quality Council, which sets priorities and chooses items to include in the Quality Plan.

⇨ *Multifunctional task teams.* Members include representatives from various areas who work on a special project, such as new product design.

☆ **Performance monitoring.** CNFD uses about 300 different measurements to track progress. These individual measurements flow up to eight key division-level pulse points:

① *Customer satisfaction*

② *Fuel reliability*

③ *Tubeshell yield*

④ *Cladding yield*

⑤ *Fuel assembly yield*

⑥ *On-time software* (This is primarily a Division headquarters measurement pertaining to documents, reports, and proposals.)

⑦ *Error-free software*

⑧ *Total quality cost*

Once a month, there is an operations meeting, which is conducted by phone. The general manager contacts plant managers, their staff, and other key people in the Division. During this phone meeting, the eight measurements described above are examined to spot trends. Managers are held accountable for those measurements that relate to their particular operations, and report on their status in each area.

"They talk about corrective actions that are necessary to remedy and problems they are having in any key area, and make the necessary improvements immediately," explains DeWitt. "All functions are interrelated, so they talk about issues that can impact many sites. It's a good way to control what's going on at all our locations."

Besides serving as an excellent vehicle for communication between plants and for providing recognition when merited, these meetings also provide a certain amount of peer pressure when performance is not as good as expected.

In addition, the measurements are posted at each location to show trends over the past three years. This also provides an incentive to those managers whose functions need to better their performance.

☆ **Customer Input.** Input from Westinghouse customers is solicited by the following means:

❑ *Fuel Users Group.* This is a steering committee of customers that meets twice annually; the Division facilitates these meetings.

> **"We've developed a culture where employees involved in quality are the norm. The Total Quality attitude is so pervasive that it's those who <u>don't</u> participate who are the exception."**

❑ *Technology Users Group.* This committee functions in much the same way the Fuel Users Group works, and was formed more recently, since the Division started offering customers additional technological products and services.

❑ *Customer audits.* Because fuel production is a highly regulated operation, customers often visit Division facilities to perform audits. A weekly schedule is distributed to upper management listing customers scheduled to visit the facility.

❑ *Customer satisfaction measurement.* This measurement is calculated monthly based on how project engineers and the field sales operation (a separate unit of Westinghouse) perceive the Division's performance. Performance is evaluated according to various criteria based on ratings of *very good, good, fair*, and *poor*. Low ratings are referred to the appropriate managers for action, and these managers are held accountable for turn-

ing the problems around. Low ratings are also referred to the general manager.

In addition, this measurement includes benchmarking, whereby senior management travels to customers' locations and customers evaluate the Division's performance. Again, ratings are *very good, good, fair,* and *poor.* The customer evaluation is factored into the first rating, which is adjusted accordingly.

☆ **Employee motivation and involvement.** The Division keeps employees at all levels motivated to work toward quality by several means:

❖ *Communication.* Through employee meetings, in-house newsletters, postings, and other means, management keeps employees informed about what is happening in the Division.

❖ *Team participation.* Working in teams makes everyone feel as if he or she is part of the company and is working toward the same goal: to satisfy customers. "A typical employee is probably working on three different team activities at a time," notes DeWitt. "This helps to break down barriers between departments. It also makes employees feel that they have *ownership* over their jobs."

❖ *Training.* Besides standard job skills training, the Division also offers training in the following areas:

➤ **Social styles.** This helps employees to understand others and to deal with them more effectively.

➤ **Leadership skills.** A one-week course is given to managers, supervisors, and professional employees on managing change, negotiation skills, and other leadership-related subjects.

❖ *Recognition.* At both corporate and division levels, Westinghouse offers various forms of recognition for employees who make a special effort to work toward Total Quality assurance. These recognition efforts include

❀ **Quality Achievement Award.** This is an annual competition in which employees nominate one another and compete at the division, business unit, and corporate levels.

❀ **Wall of Fame.** The Division uses the Quality Achievement competition as a means to recognize even more employees by choosing quality achievers at each site within the Division. Achievers are nominated by their peers and may be individuals or teams. Photos of achievers and a brief description of their accomplishments are displayed on a Wall of Fame at each site.

❋ **Certificates of Nomination.** All nominees are awarded a certificate at an annual quality awards luncheon or breakfast during which other quality awards are presented.

❋ **Creating Value Award.** This is a simple printed slip of paper that any employee can give to a co-worker who has done something extra to create value for the customer or for the organization. The donor writes the recipient's name on the slip and the reason for the award. A copy is sent to the recipient's supervisor, and some recipients are honored at the annual quality awards event.

"We let each site within the Division customize its awards according to what they feel is best for their own populations," says DeWitt. "This is because different rewards motivate different people. We give some people gift certificates to a mall. One plant may give employees cash, while another plant may award certificates to a local department store." Other awards are also given at the corporate level for licensing, patents, marketing, and other endeavors.

FOUR TOTAL QUALITY IMPERATIVES AND TWELVE CONDITIONS OF EXCELLENCE

To evaluate its progress toward its quality goals, Westinghouse measures its performance against 12 Conditions of Excellence. These conditions are grouped under four Total Quality Imperatives described as the "how to's" of performance. (In 1984, Westinghouse started to do internal benchmarking using the 12 Conditions of Excellence as criteria. Interestingly, these 12 Conditions closely coincide with the Baldrige criteria.) The Imperatives and Conditions of Excellence can best be illustrated by a pyramid design. (See Figure 2-2.)

The four Imperatives are

▲ **Customer Orientation**

▲ **Human Resource Excellence**

▲ **Product/Process Leadership**

▲ **Management Leadership**

The Conditions of Excellence that define these Imperatives are

▲ **1. Customer Orientation.** The key thrust here is satisfying customers by meeting their requirements and value expectations. Products and services must be

perceived by the customers as being first in Total Quality. To that end, these steps must be taken:

◗ The organization's value compared with its competitor's value—as defined by external customers—is to be considered and used to gain competitive advantage.

◗ *Internal* customers' perceptions are also to be measured and evaluated.

◗ Warranties on products and services are to be evaluated, and the resulting data used for improvement.

◗ Procedures for the safety and health of customers and the community are to be established, understood, and implemented.

▲ **2. Participation.** All employees are to participate in establishing and achieving Total Quality improvement goals. Managers are to lead and to encourage employee contributions. All departments are to contribute to developing and implementing the Total Quality improvement process.

> **"A typical employee is probably working on three different team activities at a time. This helps to break down barriers between departments. It also makes employees feel that they have <u>ownership</u> over their jobs."**

▲ **3. Development.** People are to be recognized as key strategic resources and, as such, are to receive the development and training they need to understand and to support the Total Quality process. They are also to receive the necessary job skills training to support the process.

▲ **4. Motivation.** Employees are to be motivated to achieve Total Quality through trust, respect, and recognition. Employees are to receive recognition regularly for contributions to Total Quality. Their managers are to personally bestow this recognition.

▲ **5. Products/Services.** Products and services are to be appropriately innovative and are to be reviewed, verified, produced, and controlled to meet customer requirements. Each area of the organization must know its value-to-cost ratios, and their products are to be made globally competitive, incorporating customer requirements as well as world-class product and service standards. Ongoing programs must exist to improve products and services. The quality of all products and services must be verified before they are delivered.

▲ **6. Processes/Procedures.** Processes and procedures used to create and deliver products and services are to be developed as an integrated, verified, and controlled system using appropriate technology and tools. Cycle time reduction is a driving force in this interactive system. Error prevention must be emphasized in process and procedure design, and processes must be controlled to be error-free. All processes and procedures are to be planned, verified before they are used, thoroughly understood, and efficiently managed. Goals and requirements set to protect employees from hazards are to be in compliance with safety, health, and environmental standards.

▲ **7. Information.** Information required to support Total Quality—and which concerns the requirements of both external and internal customers—should be clear, complete, accurate, timely, useful, accessible, and integrated with products, services, processes, and procedures. Information regarding customer requirements must be accurately communicated to all departments that must meet those requirements.

▲ **8. Suppliers.** Suppliers are to be considered *partners* that are selected, measured, controlled, and recognized on the basis of their potential and actual value contributions to meeting requirements for Total Quality. Suppliers must be given every opportunity to contribute to improvement under Total Quality imperatives.

▲ **9. Culture.** Management must establish a value system in which individual and group actions reflect a "Total Quality First" attitude and are directed to meet established world-class requirements. The organization must be bound together by the belief that Total Quality is the key to success. *"Think Total Quality—all else will follow"* describes this culture. Quality im-

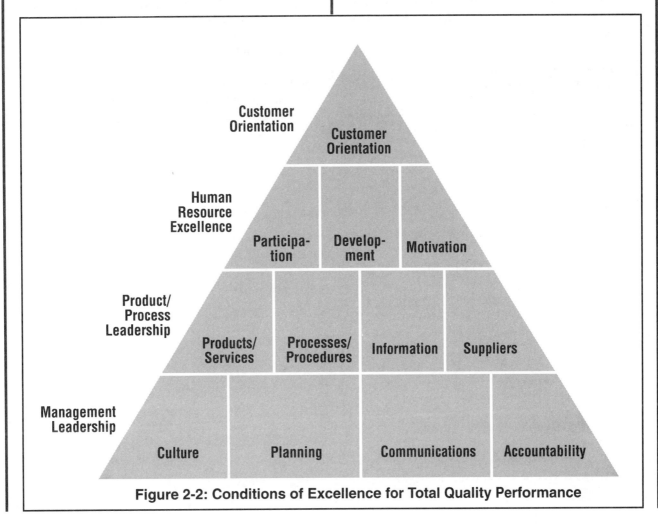

Figure 2-2: Conditions of Excellence for Total Quality Performance

provement must be seen as a long-term process, and is not ever to be compromised by short-term conditions.

▲ **10. Planning.** Those carrying out strategic business and financial planning are to recognize Total Quality as a primary, long-term business objective. Total Quality issues important to the business are always to be addressed in strategic plans. These plans are to be revised annually and used to detail formal quality improvement projects with measurable goals for each department.

▲ **11. Communications.** Both verbal and nonverbal communications are to be used by management to clearly, consistently, and forcefully communicate Total Quality policy requirements to employees. Two-way communication between management and employees is to be encouraged.

▲ **12. Accountability.** Both management and employees are to be held accountable for Total Quality performance. This performance must be measured through the setting of Total Quality improvement objectives, and subsequent progress reviews must pinpoint improvement opportunities. Measures and improvement objectives related to value/price, value/cost, and error-free performance must be visible and used in each department.

THE TOTAL QUALITY RESULTS ARE TOTALLY OUTSTANDING

DeWitt reports that the CNFD has made numerous improvements as a result of its quality efforts. These results can be seen in this table:

	1984	1990
On-time software	75 %	Close to 100%
Error-free software	94%	Close to 100%
Once-through yield		
Completed Fuel		
Assemblies	40%	90%
Finished tubing	70%	90%

Other achievements of the Division include the following:

➢ Reducing the cost/time figures by 40 percent

➢ Reducing the product development cycle from seven years (four years for development and three years for performance analysis) to a total of two years

In addition, the quality program has created Total Quality awareness at all levels. "Before, people didn't really know what upper management was focused on," DeWitt admits. "Now we have measurements posted at the group levels and the department levels. There's a much greater awareness among all employees about what's important for the business.

"Combined with the quality teams, the measurements make all employees feel that they understand the business, how they fit into the organization, and what they need to do to get results." When employees are focused in that manner, those results can be winning a Malcolm Baldrige National Quality Award, as Westinghouse learned firsthand.

Chapter Three

Malcolm Baldrige National Quality Award Winners—1989

Xerox Corporation

Through its comprehensive Leadership Through Quality process, Xerox regained marketplace strength, increased revenues, and won several quality awards—not the least of which was the Malcolm Baldrige National Quality Award, bestowed on the company in 1989.

The Xerox Corporation created the copier industry in 1959, when it introduced the first plain-paper copier. For the next 15 years, Xerox completely dominated the copier/duplicator business because it controlled the patents, and therefore, the company had no real competition.

However, in the mid-1970s, Federal Trade Commission settlements required Xerox to open international access to key patents. Of course, this also opened the floodgates for the competition. Soon, Japanese companies targeted the low-priced copiers, while IBM and Eastman Kodak competed with the higher-end equipment.

Xerox's period of unchallenged market dominance was over. And the company knew it would have to assure truly superior products and services if it was to retain its edge. By taking its time and developing a proactive Leadership Through Quality process, Xerox not only regained marketplace strength, it also won several quality awards—including the Malcolm Baldrige National Quality Award, in 1989.

BENCHMARKING PROCESS REVEALS AREAS NEEDING IMPROVEMENT

"In 1979, Xerox manufacturing and development units began to try to understand why we were not more competitive in the marketplace," says Sam M. Malone, Jr., project manager, Corporate Communications at Xerox Corporation (Webster, NY). "So these units began a benchmarking process. For Xerox, benchmarking was a process of measuring all procedures and operations against the best *external*—not internal—standards," he explains.

"Benchmarking enabled us to get some insights into strategies and improvements we needed to make in order to be more competitive. For example, through the benchmarking process, we discovered that the Japanese were *selling* their copiers for what it cost Xerox to *manufacture* them." (This enabled the Japanese to control 40 percent of the copier/duplicator market by 1980.)

Benchmarking uncovered other inefficiencies at the company. "As a result of using benchmarks, we found that we had ten times as many suppliers as our Japanese competitors had. We also found that we

employed basically twice the number of people and took twice as long to develop new products," Malone points out.

A STRATEGY TO REGAIN THAT CRITICAL COMPETITIVE EDGE

Xerox had been in a joint venture with Fuji Photo Films since 1962, but the division had not been competing effectively on the Japanese market. However, Fuji Xerox adopted a quality process, turned itself around, and won the Deming Award in 1980. David T. Kearns, then chairman and CEO of Xerox, was liaison officer to Fuji Xerox and had made over 20 trips to Japan. He noted this success and recognized that similar success was possible—and was definitely needed—throughout the corporation.

"At this time, Xerox was struggling with losing market shares, struggling with cost pressures, and struggling with not being competitive in the marketplace," recalls Malone. "So Mr. Kearns, having had experience with Fuji Xerox, said, 'Fuji is an allied industry with similar products. If a quality process worked for them, why won't it work for us?'"

Award Winning Quality

This positive, determined attitude—along with the discoveries Xerox made while benchmarking—prompted the company to develop a process that would enable it to assure top quality and delivery and recapture its marketplace position. Here are the steps the company followed in its journey toward total improvement:

■ **Form Quality of Work Life (QWL) teams.** In 1980, Xerox negotiated a contract with its manufacturing union that called for the exploration of a joint problem-solving process. "This process was designed to engage the production staff in ways to make the business more effective and to gather ideas for improvement," reports Malone.

"But those were basically stand-alone efforts in our Webster, New York manufacturing plant and were not related, not integrated, and certainly did not go broad-based across the organization."

■ **Increase the number of QWL Teams and decrease the number of suppliers.** In 1981, the number of Quality of Work Life Teams continued to grow in the manufacturing division. Xerox began reducing its production supplier base, which then numbered 5,000 suppliers.

Xerox also began to conduct seminars across the country for its suppliers to train them in statistical process and quality control. Eventually, fewer than 500 production suppliers were being used by the company.

■ **Start up employee involvement (EI) groups in product development areas.** The following year, in 1982, the employee involvement process spread to the product development organizations in Webster and Henrietta, New York.

> **Leadership Through Quality was a long-term process meant to change the way Xerox people worked and managed so they could continuously improve the way they met the requirements of their customers.**

■ **Implement the just in time (JIT) process.** In less than one year, in 1982, JIT at Xerox was recognized as saving the company $1 million in inventory costs.

■ **Initiate a quality leadership process.** Early in 1983, 25 key senior corporate managers at Xerox met in their training center right outside of Washington, D.C. "This group became the designers of the quality process inside Xerox," Malone reports. "That process was titled, 'Leadership Through Quality.'"

This was a long-term process meant to change the way Xerox people worked and managed so they could *continuously improve* the way they met the requirements of their customers.

"There were some fundamental stakes in the ground put down at that meeting," explains Malone. These were the resolutions the group developed concerning Xerox's quality effort:

✪ *It was to be a worldwide process.*

✪ *It would involve all employees.*

✪ *It would use a common approach to quality improvement and problem-solving.*

✪ *Every employee would be thoroughly trained.*

✪ *Training would cascade down through the organization, focusing on managers as the training conduits.*

This strategy integrated existing QWL and EI teams into a more comprehensive, corporatewide, worldwide effort.

■ **Plan the quality process slowly and carefully.** "The management team spent around a year and a half developing our Leadership Through Quality process," explains Malone. "The old attitude had been, 'ready, fire, aim,'" he concedes. "This time, however, we were really taking care to 'ready, aim, and then fire.' And we didn't fire until we felt sure the aim was right."

With this in mind, the management team was certain of several factors as it worked on its plans:

★ **The quality strategy was going to be a *process*, not a program.** Xerox would not call its quality effort a *program*, because a program has a beginning and an end. "We would instead call it a *process*, because a process is ongoing," Malone stresses.

★ **The company was making a *long-term* commitment.** "We did not get sick overnight; therefore we did not expect that we would get well overnight," Malone asserts.

"We spent a lot of time researching existing approaches to quality," he continues. "We adopted approaches from others so that they would fit our culture and our needs. Once the elements were agreed upon, the training team designed a training program to meet those needs."

■ **Develop a specific quality policy and identify change mechanisms necessary to fulfill it.** During its planning period, the executives developed the Xerox Quality Policy, which says:

Xerox is a quality company. Quality is the basic business principle for Xerox. Quality means providing our external and internal customers with innovative products and services that fully satisfy their requirements. Quality improvement is the job of every Xerox employee.

The management team recognized that fulfilling this policy's requirements would necessitate an enormous change in the Xerox culture. So they laid out a five-year strategy to accomplish this change and identified six change mechanisms they would use to support the cultural change being undertaken:

★ **Management behavior and actions:** Managers were to lead the change by practicing the principles of

Leadership Through Quality *day in and day out.*

★ **Transition teams:** These teams were to guide the changes and to make sure the implementation was consistent across the organization.

★ **Standards and measurements:** These were to provide Xerox people with new ways of assessing and performing their work and solving problems, and it included a nine-step quality improvement process; competitive benchmarking; an emphasis on error prevention and doing things right the first time; and techniques for determining the cost of quality.

★ **Training:** Every Xerox staffer was to be given an understanding of Leadership Through Quality and a working knowledge of the tools and techniques for quality improvement. The training would be delivered in "family groups" consisting of a manager and the people who reported directly to him or her. It was to include application of the newly learned tools on a work group project. Also, the training was to "cascade" downward throughout the organization.

★ **Recognition and rewards:** To encourage and motivate Xerox people to practice the behaviors of Leadership Through Quality, some form of recognition was to be given. This could be in the form of a simple thank-you or a cash bonus.

★ **Communication:** All Xerox people were to be kept informed of the objectives and priorities of the corporation and of their work groups. Both formal and informal media were to be used, including films, company magazines and newsletters, and staff meetings.

> **"The old attitude was 'ready, fire, aim.' This time, however, we were really taking care to 'ready, aim, and then fire.' And we didn't fire until we felt sure the aim was right."**

■ **Roll out the Leadership Through Quality process.** "Early in 1984, we started the rollout of our Leadership Through Quality process," reports Malone. "Training started at the very top, with Mr. Kearns, the CEO, personally training his staff. From there, each level of management trained its staff and it cascaded down the line until every employee, worldwide, was trained. All employees were given a common set of tools to work with: a common language for quality, and a common approach through two models; the quality improvement process and the problem-solving process. (See Figures 3-1 and 3-2.)

"We completed our initial worldwide training effort in 1988, when every one of our 100,000 employees had been trained," Malone reports. "After the training effort was completed, we could pull any employee—an engineer from Holland, a designer from France, a service engineer from California, a sales representative from Texas, and a production worker from New York—into a conference room, and they would all be able to walk into that room and use the same process to tackle the business issues that caused them to come together," he asserts.

■ **Continue to increase the number of worldwide problem-solving teams.** Both the QWL and EI Teams were pulled into the mainstream. By the end of 1984, there were more than 300 teams actively involved in problem-solving. In 1985, all teams became known as Quality Improvement Teams. By 1986, 2,500 Quality Improvement Teams were solving problems worldwide.

INCREASED EFFECTIVENESS LEADS TO BALDRIGE APPLICATION—AND XEROX WINS

In 1987, an Act of Congress established the Malcolm Baldrige National Quality Award. (See Chapter One.) Of course, Xerox had started its internal quality revolution in 1983—long before the establishment of the Baldrige Award. However, Xerox did not apply during the first year of the Award's existence. In late 1988, Xerox's senior management team made the decision to prepare an application for possible submission in 1989.

"It was not a foregone conclusion that we would actually submit the application," says Malone. "We positioned our efforts as a 'learning experience.' We said that 10 percent of our effort was to win the Baldrige and 90 percent was to learn and to educate ourselves. Further, we said that the application effort would cover our Xerox Business Products and Systems organization, which had 50,200 employees. Our second business, Xerox Financial Services, was not covered by our application."

A National Quality Award office was established to lead the effort. "Because the application covered such a broad range of functions, we formed a core team of 20 people whose job it was to do the research and then to write the application," Malone explains.

"The team consisted of a multifunctional cross sec-

continued on page 55

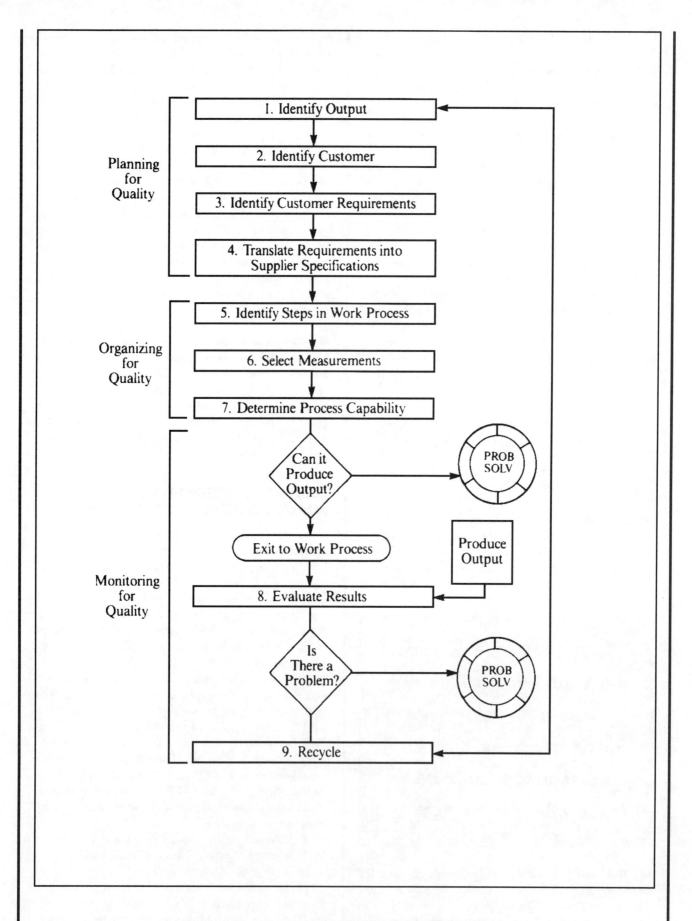

Figure 3-1: Xerox Quality Improvement Process

continued from page 53

tion of the corporation. It included finance people, a union member, and people from personnel, sales, service, manufacturing and development, and others. Members varied as the team entered various stages of the process. Most team members were middle managers with an average of 20 years with the corporation.

"The team first had to learn what the Baldrige was about, and then draft our application. (It went through four drafts.) It was understood that if Xerox decided to submit the application, this team would also plan for a potential site visit. Following that, the team members were to deliver an assessment report to management based on their findings when writing the application and preparing for the site visit. This report would be the items that management would focus on for continuing the improvement of our internal quality process," Malone explains.

The decision was made in early April 1989 to submit the Xerox application. It was submitted on May 1, 1989. (Xerox was one of 40 companies submitting an application in 1989.)

On May 28, Xerox received notification that its application had been judged complete and was one of 23 in the manufacturing category to undergo a preliminary screening. This screening, conducted by a team of examiners, was based on an evaluation of 16 of the 44 questions responded to in the application.

On July 10, Xerox was notified that its application would move into the second stage of the review process, which meant that its entire application would now be evaluated.

Xerox was notified that it would receive a site visit. On August 17, 1989, the company was told that it had been selected to receive a site visit the week of September 17. A team of five members of the board of examiners conducted the site visit on Monday, Tuesday, and Wednesday of that week. They were accompanied by two observers representing the National Institute of Standards and Technology (NIST).

In those three days, the examiners visited a total of five different sites located in New York, Colorado, and California. Their task was to verify the contents of the application and to check the extent to which the company's quality efforts were deployed overall in the Business Products and Systems Organization. To accomplish this, the examiners talked with three different groups of employees. These groups were the following:

✶ **Category Teams.** Groups of five to eight employees met with the examiners to answer specific questions on each of the seven categories covered in the Baldrige application.

✶ **Employee Involvement and Quality Im-**

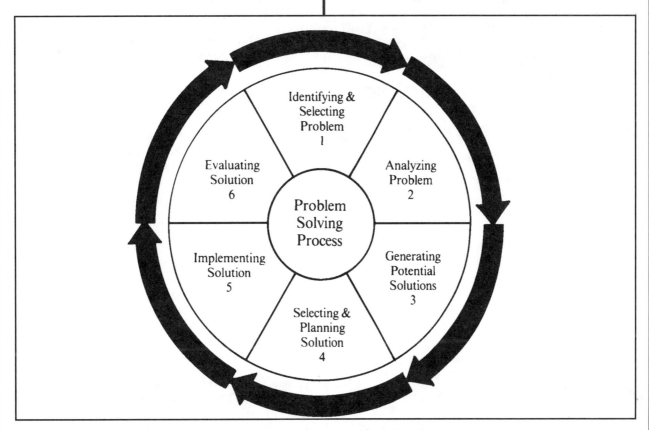

Figure 3-2: Xerox Problem Solving Process

provement Teams. Examiners met with these teams to discuss their projects, processes, and results.

✮ **Individual employees.** "The examiners requested that they have lunch in the cafeteria unescorted during their visit," says Malone. "Examiners went through the cafeteria line and chose whom they would sit with. They would talk to the employees individually about the quality process, what they were doing to support it, and how they controlled their processes, among other significant factors.

"Many times, the examiners stopped people in the hall and talked to them or they got on an elevator and pushed the button for the floor they wanted," Malone notes. "They would get off the elevator, introduce themselves, and proceed to ask questions. They were free to wander anyplace they wanted to. All in all, they talked to over 425 Xerox employees during their three-day site visit."

> **"It was not a foregone conclusion that we would actually submit the application. We positioned our efforts as a 'learning experience.' We said that 10 percent of our effort was to win the Baldrige and 90 percent was to learn and to educate ourselves."**

Following their visit to Xerox, the examiners submitted their site-visit report to the panel of nine judges. The first week in October, the judges met to review all the site-visit reports and to select the recipients of the 1989 awards.

Of course, the rest was history: Xerox *did* win the 1989 Malcolm Baldrige National Quality Award. On November 2, 1989, at the Department of Commerce, President Bush presented the Award to Xerox's Business Products and Systems Unit and Milliken & Company. (The judges did not feel that any of the 1989 applicants in the service and small business categories met their stringent criteria, so no Awards were bestowed in these areas.)

THE "RACE FOR QUALITY" HAS NO FINISH LINE

According to Xerox President and CEO David Kearns, "The race for quality has no finish line." He reinforced that belief in his acceptance remarks at the Department of Commerce.

Kearns said, "Based on our findings during the application process, we have already made changes, and more will come in our ongoing quest for continuous quality improvement and customer satisfaction. This moment is but a milestone in the Xerox continuing quality drive."

After Xerox accepted its Award, the team that originally wrote the application and coordinated the site visit drafted its assessment report. It noted more than 500 areas for further improvement. The team also developed a set of 51 action considerations for management's review that would enable Xerox to advance its "race" for improved quality and increased customer satisfaction.

"The senior management team accepted this report and took ownership of it," says Malone. "Mr. Kearns is on record as saying that this report is worth millions of dollars to Xerox because it really sets down what we need to do over the long haul to substantially improve the corporation."

THE SUCCESS IS SHARED FAR AND WIDE

"The Baldrige Award was really created to do three things," explains Malone. These are:

❶ *To focus America's attention on the need for improved quality*

❷ *To recognize organizations that had achieved outstanding results using quality improvement processes*

❸ *To share their successful strategies with others*

"We have been very open in our sharing process," Malone notes. "We have shared our ideas with more than 110,000 businesspeople across the United States since winning the Baldrige Award in 1989.

"In 1990, we averaged 35 calls a day. And in 1991, we averaged 25 calls a day. These calls range from requests for our CEO to talk at functions to questions on how we went about winning the Baldrige Award."

QUALITY HAS MANY REWARDS— HAPPY CUSTOMERS IS NUMBER ONE

"Since 1985, we've had a 41 percent improvement in the ratings our customers give us in regard to their satisfaction with our products and services," Malone reports. "We mail about 40,000 surveys a month to our customers and ask them to tell us how we are doing.

"In September 1990, we implemented the Xerox Total Satisfaction Guarantee, which basically says that if you buy a Xerox product and you are unhappy with it, for any reason, within the first three years of ownership, let us know and we will replace it free of charge. Obviously, if we didn't have a comfort level about the quality of our products and services, we could not enter into that kind of agreement," explains Malone.

> **"The Baldrige process is valuable because it forces you to look at your company the way the _customer_ sees it—not the way _you_ think it is."**

Other benefits Xerox has enjoyed from its Leadership Through Quality process include:

★ **_Increased revenues:_** In 1990, revenues grew to $17.6 billion; earnings increased 11 percent.

★ **_Product kudos:_** Buyers Laboratory, Inc., named Xerox as having the "most outstanding product line of 1990."

★ **_Additional awards:_** In 1983, the Rank Xerox Venray manufacturing facility was given the CIMEI Quality Award by the Dutch government. The following year, the Rank Xerox Limited Micheldean manufacturing facility received the British Quality Award. Many more quality awards were given to affiliates abroad in the following years. Xerox won additional national quality awards in Mexico and Australia in 1990, bringing to _nine_ the total number of national quality awards won since 1980 by Xerox operating companies worldwide.

THE "RACE WITHOUT A FINISH LINE" KEEPS ON GOING

"The number-one corporate objective is customer satisfaction," stresses Malone. "Xerox is preoccupied with the customer. The Baldrige process is valuable because it forces you to look at your company the way the _customer_ sees it—not the way _you_ think it is.

"The quality race is a very frustrating race," he concedes. "The further you go, the more you realize how far you still have to go. That is why our president and CEO Mr. Kearns said at the Baldrige Awards ceremony, 'we're in a race without a finish line.' You have to continue to tighten up your processes and to _continuously improve_ if you are to remain competitive in today's global marketplace."

Milliken & Company

This top textile company's Pursuit Of Excellence (POE) process and Corrective Action teams helped lead it to a Baldrige win in 1989.

Headquartered in Spartanburg, South Carolina, the 124-year-old privately owned Milliken & Company has 14,000 "associates" employed primarily at 47 manufacturing facilities in the United States. Milliken's 28 businesses produce more than 48,000 different textile and chemical products—ranging from apparel fabrics and automotive fabrics to specialty chemicals and floor coverings. Annual sales exceed $1 billion.

In 1981, senior management implemented Milliken's Pursuit of Excellence (POE), a commitment to customer satisfaction that pervades all company levels. This pursuit has led to improvements in what most competitors had already considered an enviable record

of quality and performance. Since the early 1980s, productivity has increased 42 percent.

Teams are the hallmark of the Milliken quality improvement process. In 1988, 1,600 Corrective Action Teams formed to address specific manufacturing or other internal business problems, 200 Supplier Action Teams worked to improve Milliken's relationship with its suppliers, and nearly 500 teams responded to the needs and aims of customers. Quality improvement measures are solidly based on factual information that is contained in an array of standardized databases accessible from all Milliken facilities.

Most manufacturing processes are under the scrutiny of real-time monitoring systems that detect errors and help pinpoint their causes. Milliken's successful push for quality improvement has allowed it to increase U.S. sales and enter foreign markets.

Chapter Four

Malcolm Baldrige National Quality Award Winners—1990

Cadillac Motor Car Company

This company once suffered from ineffective planning and declining sales—until it used the power of a Simultaneous Engineering Pyramid to turn itself around and become a Baldrige winner.

In 1985, Cadillac Motor Car Company, a Division of General Motors (Detroit, MI), reacted to the forecast of a fuel shortage (that didn't materialize) and new emission controls (that did) by downsizing its cars. As a result of acting too fast to adjust to what it believed would be the new marketplace, the company misjudged its customers' expectations—and sales fell dramatically.

Just five years later, however, Cadillac had turned itself around so completely that it won a Malcolm Baldrige National Quality Award—and regained the confidence of its customers.

"Typically, most companies start looking downstream when business isn't going well; top management wants to fix the plant or the manufacturing process," explains Rosetta Riley, director of Customer Satisfaction. "However, our top management was willing to make changes from the top level down.

"We all knew that our cars weren't being accepted in the marketplace as we thought they should be. We had discussions at top levels about what changes we could make to turn our business around.

"In 1985 and 1986, 1,600 of our employees spent four days listening to Dr. W. Edwards Deming, the quality 'guru' who sparked the Japanese quality revolution. Dr. Deming doesn't really tell you how to get to quality. Basically, he reminds management that *they* are the reason their company doesn't have quality," Riley says. "We felt that his message was outstanding: He really makes you aware of where your problem is and where the solution has to start."

The year 1985 also brought something else to Cadillac: *simultaneous engineering,* a philosophy that affects how products are designed, engineered, and manufactured. Simultaneous engineering is defined as "a process in which appropriate disciplines are committed to work interactively to conceive, approve, develop, and implement product programs that meet predetermined Cadillac objectives."

Under this new approach, the company would reject the sequential design, manufacturing, and marketing of cars, where a new model was passed along from department to department. Instead, teamwork, communication, and group decision-making would be emphasized in the manufacturing process. "We chose the team approach because we recognized that our value base was our people," says Riley. "We needed to put a process in place that would allow our people to work to their maximum.

"We also focused on the voice of the customer, using quality function deployment to translate that voice into technical and manufacturing specifications."

ERECTING THE PYRAMID: A MONUMENT TO EXCELLENCE

As a first step, management adopted the pyramid as the symbol of simultaneous engineering (see Figure 4-1). Here is an explanation of each "building block" of the pyramid:

✪ **Cadillac Motor Car Executive Staff:** At the foundation of the pyramid is the Cadillac Motor Car Executive Staff, which supports and nurtures the process by establishing policy and direction.

✪ **Steering Committee:** Next on the pyramid is the Steering Committee, which is composed of managers who report directly to the Executive Staff. Their role is to plan and implement simultaneous engineering policy and direction, with core members meeting weekly to discuss issues and future strategies.

✪ **Vehicle Teams and Vehicle System Management Teams:** In the next slot are Vehicle Teams, which are responsible for managing all steps of product development for each vehicle program. They manage three key elements of a vehicle program: timing, profitability, and continuous improvement of the vehicle's quality, reliability, durability, and performance. On the same level of the pyramid as the Vehicle Teams are the Vehicle System Management Teams. Their role is to manage each of the six specific vehicle systems (such as Exterior Component/Body Mechanical, Chassis/Powertrain Application, and Seats and Interior Trim), and they work in partnership with the Vehicle Teams to develop program definitions and objectives for each model year.

Award Winning Quality

✪ **Product Development and Improvement Teams:** The next level of the pyramid is composed of the Product Development and Improvement Teams, which are responsible for the design of components that make up the six major systems. These groups have "cradle-to-grave" responsibility for the production and continuous improvement of parts for their assigned portion of the automobile design. Suppliers work as full business partners with these groups and help make decisions on design, materials, and manufacturing processes.

✪ **Assembly Operators:** Third from the top of the pyramid are Assembly Operators, who work with the teams to solve problems and provide insight for future

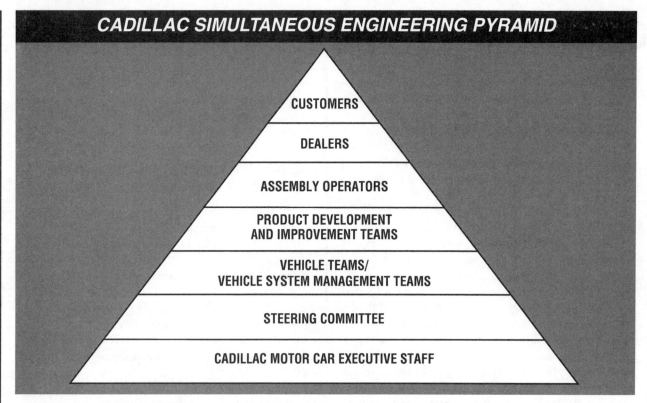

CADILLAC SIMULTANEOUS ENGINEERING PYRAMID

CUSTOMERS

DEALERS

ASSEMBLY OPERATORS

PRODUCT DEVELOPMENT
AND IMPROVEMENT TEAMS

VEHICLE TEAMS/
VEHICLE SYSTEM MANAGEMENT TEAMS

STEERING COMMITTEE

CADILLAC MOTOR CAR EXECUTIVE STAFF

Figure 4-1: Cadillac Simultaneous Engineering Pyramid

designs.

✪ **Auto Dealers:** Second from the top are Auto Dealers, who give Cadillac feedback on customer concerns.

✪ **Customers:** Resting atop the pyramid in their rightful place are the Customers who ultimately purchase the product that all these other people are attempting to deliver in a quality fashion.

GAINING CRUCIAL CUSTOMER INPUT AND ASSISTANCE

Cadillac recognizes the value of its customers, as evidenced by the fact that the company places them at the top of its pyramid. But it's not just customers' business Cadillac is interested in: A large part of the value of the customer is what Cadillac can learn from them to make improvements.

"We implement several strategies to hear the voice of the customer," says Riley. Here's a look at these strategies:

➤ *Outside marketing firms do written surveys.*
➤ *Customers and noncustomers evaluate fiberglass models of proposed car designs at clinics.*
➤ *Dealers give feedback on customer suggestions for improvement or acceptance of designs.*
➤ *Salaried and hourly employees speak directly with customers, either by direct phone calls, "working the floor" at auto shows, attending*

the clinics where customers evaluate the fiberglass models, or by visiting auto dealers.

All this attention to simultaneous engineering and the voice of the customer paid off for Cadillac. "In 1989, we were named among the top five automobile manufacturers in the world," Riley reports, "and we were the only domestic automobile manufacturer so named.

"Around this time, we got word of the Malcolm Baldrige Award. We decided to take a look at the application because we heard that the assessment method was excellent. At this point, our strategy was not to win the award, but to assess our own processes and systems and to improve them where needed. We submitted our application to the Baldrige committee.

"In 1989, we got an on-site visit from the Baldrige examining committee, but we did not win," says Riley. "But we did so well that we decided to go after the Award again in 1990—and we won."

It isn't as easy as it may sound, however. "Most people assume that you go after the Baldrige Award and start putting improvement processes together then," explains Riley. "However, that's too late.

"We started the quest to turn our company around in 1985, and that's when our processes began to be put into place. The Baldrige self-examination strategy helped us polish these processes and make internal improvements that not only improved our quality assurance efforts further but also helped us win the 1990 Baldrige Award."

Employee Suggestion System Helps Cadillac Improve Quality, Cut Costs—and More

One of the secrets to Cadillac's quality success is the company's strong employee suggestion program. Cadillac knows that the best source of ideas for improving a company's processes are the people who actually work with those processes.

"Improved quality, cost savings, and reduced accidents can all be attributed to the ideas we've received through our suggestion program," asserts James Klee, divisional administrator of Suggestions for Flint Automotive Division, Buick/Oldsmobile/Cadillac Group of General Motors (Flint, MI). The suggestion program at General Motors was established 50 years ago.

General Motors is one of approximately 1,000 member companies belonging to the National Association of Suggestion Systems (NASS). In 1990, NASS members received more than one million suggestions that saved their companies $2.3 billion. Of the 1,027,364 suggestions submitted (which equals 11 suggestions for every 100 eligible employees), a total of 328,326 were adopted.

"Our suggestion program provides a corporatewide method for employees to submit their ideas for improvements—either individually, or in groups or teams—for quality, cost savings, and safety," Klee explains. "Over the last five years, quality has assumed a much greater role than it had in the past. Our program was considered more of a cost-saving program—and it still presents substantial savings to General Motors—but the *quality* aspect has increased significantly.

"Evidence of this can be found in the fact that our Cadillac Division won the 1990 Malcolm Baldrige National Quality Award," Klee notes. "Now more than ever, our employees understand the importance of quality and its role in a globally competitive environment."

WHAT CAN YOU GAIN FROM A FORMAL SUGGESTION SYSTEM?

"There are several good reasons every company should institute a suggestion program in their operations," Klee asserts. Here are just a few of the benefits you can gain from a formal suggestion system:

✯ **Effective problem-solving.** "The most obvious reason you should use a suggestion program is that you'll improve your product, save money, have more efficient processes, and so on," says Klee. "There are *thousands* of untapped ideas in the minds of employees. The companies that listen to these ideas and encourage them will be the companies that succeed.

"The people who understand a specific operation the best are the employees performing that function," he adds. "If a better way is going to be found to do a job, it's generally going to be found by the people doing that job. So you want employees to feel free to submit their ideas."

✯ **Systematic evaluation of ideas.** "A suggestion program is so beneficial because it provides a formalized structure to make sure that ideas are looked at and evaluated," says Klee. "If you have a system where ideas are looked at only casually, they're often not looked at *appropriately*. Or suggesters are not guaranteed that their ideas will always be evaluated properly. "A formalized suggestion program is, basically, a contract between the suggesters and the company that mandates that the ideas *will be* examined and evaluated."

✯ **Enhanced employee involvement, ownership, and morale.** "Employees like to feel that they're part of the company," Klee points out. "They sincerely *want* to be involved in the business. Having a formalized suggestion program provides a mechanism for that to happen and to recognize those employees for their participation.

"For a suggestion program to be truly effective, it is exceptionally important that all levels of management support it," Klee stresses. "They must support employees' submitting suggestions and be involved in the process by honestly responding to the ideas they offer.

"Our suggestion program works well throughout the entire company, but some of our plants do *exceedingly* well as far as participation rate, adoption rate, and volume of suggestions are concerned," he continues. "Generally speaking, those plants that consistently have a high volume of suggestions have strong support from *the entire organization*, and that helps generate further ideas."

Quality managers, production managers, and other appropriate staffers must evaluate employees' suggestions and determine whether they are viable or unworkable. Then, they must assist in implementing those ideas. "Our quality people are involved with suggestions every single day," Klee notes. "In a couple of our plants, we had significant problems in quality control—and employees' ideas helped solve those problems."

➤ *Suggestions in Action* ➔ Klee cites an actual instance at General Motors where the suggestion system came to the rescue and saved the day. "Two years ago, we had a quality problem at one of our plants," he recalls. "It was a minor problem, but due to our heavy emphasis on quality, we were even considering shutting down that plant if the problem was not resolved within the next few days. Of course, when you shut down an assembly plant, you lose a lot of money. Plus, employees' jobs are affected, and your customers don't get their cars when they want them. It's a bad situation all the way around.

"The quality people at this plant realized they had to come up with way to get this problem solved *immediately*, so they had a meeting of all the quality control people, along with the plant manager and a few other key staff members," Klee continues. "At this meeting, they decided to use the suggestion program as a way to specifically address the problem. They also made a commitment to get *all* suggestions answered *within 24 hours*—which is unheard of in the suggestion industry.

"The plant quickly created a flyer explaining the situation and delivered it to all the departments," Klee continues. "The departments, in turn, communicated the message to all the employees. Many good suggestions came in. However, one particular suggestion was not only evaluated and answered within 24 hours; it was also *implemented*, and the problem was resolved within a couple of days."

Although many good ideas *are* generated to solve problems that arise, Klee notes that most employees' suggestions are geared not toward problem-solving but toward *making improvements*. "The basis of most of the ideas we receive involve improving something," he states. "Things are fine, but employees come up with ways to make them *even better*."

MAKING A SUGGESTION PLAN WORK FOR YOU

An employee suggestion program can only be successful if those implementing it keep several factors foremost in mind:

✮ **Make sure employees know how the suggestion plan works.** Don't assume that you can receive detailed, constructive suggestions from employees who are uninformed of what tack those suggestions should take, how they're to be submitted, and what criteria determine acceptance or rejection, Klee cautions. You must work out every aspect of your suggestion plan in advance and inform your employees about how the plan works. You must also keep them up-to-date on job problems needing solutions, and the direct, personal role they can play in the company's success.

✮ **Respond to suggestions promptly.** "If you want to have a successful suggestion program, respond to the suggestions that you receive right away," advises Klee. "By responding to the employees promptly, you will stimulate them to submit *more* ideas. The longer your processing time—and evaluation and recognition process—is, the less success you're going to have with your program.

"Whenever a company's suggestion program is not successful, I always recommend that people at the company respond more quickly to their people's suggestions," Klee stresses. "Promoting the program by publicizing it with posters, flyers, and articles in your company's newsletter is good, but that is only a slight stimulus. If you don't answer your people promptly, it's all going to fall on deaf ears no matter how much promotion you do."

✮ **Examine suggestions thoroughly.** "If you don't thoroughly evaluate employees' suggestions, you'll kill your program and deprive your company of a lot of benefits that it might otherwise have found useful. Quite frequently, a suggestion program just being initiated in a company is a lot more successful than the company anticipated it would be. The volume of suggestions is much higher than projected, so there's a tendency to gloss over them. However, if you don't really examine the ideas and give them a fair evaluation, your program will not be successful," Klee stresses.

✮ **Explain why ideas are rejected.** "By taking the time to explain which ideas are or are not accepted and why, you educate your people on what constitutes good suggestions *and* continually promote the suggestion system," Klee explains. "The more quickly you respond and the more you educate employees, the better the quality of suggestions that will be coming in—and the higher your adoption rate will be."

Klee concludes that there *is* a direct correlation between a high volume of suggestions and quality. "A large percentage of all the suggestions we receive at our division—possibly as high as 70 percent of our suggestions—involve quality," he points out. "The suggestion program has been—and will continue to be—a key element in Flint Automotive Division's and General Motors' meeting their goal of satisfying customers with products that are both world-class in quality and a great value."

Federal Express Corporation

A 10-step Baldrige self-analysis and self-improvement process and 12 Quality Indicators are the catalysts that helped this top-notch organization deliver superior quality—and become the first Baldrige Award winner in the service category.

The first Malcolm Baldrige National Quality Awards were given in 1988. However, it wasn't until 1990 that a large service company captured one of the prized awards. It's not too surprising that the winner was Federal Express, an organization that's been setting standards for service quality since its inception.

Starting in 1973 with eight aircraft, the company rapidly expanded its overnight airborne delivery service to a fleet of 200 aircraft (in 1991), while maintaining customer satisfaction levels of better than 95 percent. However, its sustained success has never allowed Federal Express to sit back and take it easy; the organization is always looking for ways to improve even *more*—which is where the Baldrige Award came in.

"Our approach to the Baldrige Award was one of self-analysis and self-improvement," explains John R. West, manager of Corporate Quality Improvement for Federal Express Corporation (Memphis, TN). "We recognized that the Award process was a great blueprint for quality."

A TEN-STEP PROCESS FOR IMPROVEMENT

With self-assessment and self-betterment foremost in mind, Federal Express took the following 10 steps, using the Baldrige application as a quality tool:

① **Have each division apply for the Baldrige individually.** "Each of our divisions applied as a separate entity," West explains. "As their first step in the process, Corporate assigned the division heads the responsibility of appointing a managing director to lead their individual application processes.

"The idea was to take the completed division applications and compile them into one corporate application. While doing this, each division was going through a valuable self-analysis and self-improvement process."

② **Have each division submit an action plan for improvement.** By August 1, 1989, the divisions were ready for the second step," relates West. "They were asked to submit an action plan telling the chief executive and chief operating officers what they were going to do to close any gaps between Baldrige Award requirements and their actual performance."

③ **Bring in expert help.** In the middle of writing the applications, some people had trouble understanding the exact meaning of some questions and how the scoring worked. "To get answers to these questions we brought in a consultant who was an authorized Baldrige examiner," says West. "Our purpose in hiring him was to make sure we were on the right track, we did *not* employ him to write our exam for us or to do our work for us."

④ **Hold an application workshop.** The consultant held a workshop for key players in each of the divisions participating in the completion of the application guidelines. Approximately 30 people spent a day and a half together getting answers to their questions and ensuring that they were on the right track.

⑤ **Make some needed changes.** "As a result of the workshop, we realized that we had to change our course a little bit," says West. "We now understood the scoring, and we found that we had not always understood exactly what answers the questions were looking for.

"For example, if the application asks for charts, graphs, or trends, that's what it means. Notice the three significant things they focus on in the application guidelines: *approach*, *deployment*, and *results*. Include these factors in your answers whenever it's appropriate.

"Because of this new understanding, we extended the deadline for the divisions' completion of their work by two months. That was a turning point."

⑥ **Have the divisions polish their applications.** Most divisions finished writing up their applications by the end of January, with the rest finishing up in February.

⑦ **Write the corporate application.** West and six vice presidents led teams that compiled the division applications into the corporate application, working category by category. "Divisions sent their experts to the seven category meetings to share their information and help write the corporate application," he notes.

⑧ **Have an objective outside observer critique the corporate application.** "Once we had the rough draft for each of the seven Baldrige categories completed, we submitted the written manuscript to a consultant and asked him to give it a hard critique," West reports. "We wanted to know everything that was not good in the application."

⑨ Have professional writers help with the final application. "After we got the consultant's feedback, we had professional, in-house writers write the final application," West explains. "That way, we had someone who was both knowledgeable about the company *and* had expertise in writing.

"The Baldrige application questions are very thorough," he points out. "One of the biggest points I can make is that people should be sure to answer the questions *directly*. That was the biggest advantage of having professional writers help write the final draft for us."

⑩ Send in the application. "It wasn't until a consultant told us that we had a good chance of having a site visit [by Baldrige examiners] that we made the decision to send in our application," says West. "Our main intent all along was self-analysis that would lead to self-improvement. We wanted to be good enough to warrant a site visit before we threw our hat into the ring in 1990."

> **"The idea was to take the completed division applications and compile them into one corporate application. While doing this, each division was going through a valuable self-analysis and self-improvement process."**

Of course, Federal Express *did* eventually receive a site visit. This is an intensive examination by a team of four to six people, a process that can last up to four days. The examiners rate the applications based on their observations, and then give their site visit report to a panel of judges, which selects the winners.

A DOZEN SERVICE QUALITY INDICATORS HELP KEEP EFFORTS ON TRACK

On December 13, 1990, company representatives accepted the Baldrige Award from President George Bush during a ceremony at the Department of Commerce Building. Since receiving the Award, Federal Express has shared nonproprietary information about its quality improvement process with other companies, government agencies, and education divisions. Federal Express also enlightens visitors at weekly quality forums.

One thing visitors learn when they attend these quality forums is that the company has always taken quality seriously, as evidenced by its quality measuring system.

"We have what we call a Service Quality Indicator," explains West. "This is analogous to Motorola's Six Sigma program (see section on Motorola, a 1988 Baldrige winner, in Chapter Two), which helped it win the Baldrige Award previously."

Sigma is a statistical symbol: The higher the sigma number, the fewer the failures or variations, and the better the quality. "We did not use the Six Sigma program as a model when we developed this," West says. "Our Service Quality Indicator was based on our own complaint-handling system. Our purpose was to reduce the actual number of mistakes and failures made in a year, despite volume growth."

The Service Quality Indicator is based on these 12 service components:

➤ *Wrong day, late delivery*

➤ *Right day, late delivery*

➤ *Invoice adjustments* (When people call to ask that their invoices be adjusted, it is treated and measured as a failure.)

➤ *Trace requests* (When a customer calls in to track a package and the information is not on the computer, it is treated as a failure.)

➤ *Lost packages*

➤ *Damaged packages*

➤ *Overgoods* (This concerns lost-and-found items: When the identification comes off a package, it is sent to the Overgoods Department, where an attempt is made to find out who the package belongs to.)

➤ *Missed pickups* (This occurs when a customer calls to have a package picked up today, and the package is still sitting there tomorrow.)

➤ *Complaints reopened* (When a customer calls back about a complaint that was considered "closed"—or resolved—the complaint is "reopened.")

➤ *Abandoned calls* (This term is used when a customer hangs up because his or her call isn't answered within ten seconds or two rings.)

➤ *Missing proof of delivery* (Federal Express promises that on each and every invoice it will have proof of delivery. This includes the name of the person receiving the package, the date, and the time received. If this information is not on the invoice, it is treated as a failure.)

➤ *International* (This refers to any operations that are offshore of the United States.)

"The components for International are much the same as for Domestic, but they measure their own Service Quality Indicator," explains West. "We just compile the entire International Service Quality Indicator into this one category and include it as one of *our* 12 components.

"Our five-year goal on the Service Quality Indicator is to have only one tenth of the actual number of failures at the end of the fifth year that we had at the beginning of the first year—despite an annual growth of usually about 20 percent."

But just how does Federal Express determine how well it is doing in each area? It has very extensive automatic tracking systems. For instance, consider the two methods used for monitoring late deliveries:

✧ The courier time cards require couriers to code and note any late deliveries. This information goes into a database each day, so by the next morning, the company knows the service level from the previous day.

✧ Because the delivery information goes onto each invoice, it is therefore on the billing database, which provides a second report on service-quality levels.

EMPLOYEE SATISFACTION RANKS UP THERE WITH CUSTOMER SATISFACTION

As customer satisfaction is of vital importance to Federal Express, so is *employee* satisfaction. After all, there's a strong connection between the two: If the people who are expected to provide quality service to customers are unhappy, they aren't really going to be able to provide the level of service the company expects—and the customers demand.

West explains that Federal Express took special steps to keep employees content during the Baldrige qualification process. "During the 15 months we worked on this, we spread the work out so that it was a team effort. This meant that there would be no pressure put on any one group or individual at the company. Some divisions put in a lot of hours, but they found that it was a rewarding team experience," he notes.

To make sure the company is generally on track regarding worker satisfaction, "we hold an anonymous employee survey each year," says West. "This is a man-

datory survey, so the percentage of returns is high—and the anonymity lets employees tell us what they actually feel. The goal is to have our employees feel as satisfied as they were last year (provided, of course, that we did *well* last year). If we did *not* do well, our goal is to make them *more* satisfied than they were last year."

> **"Our five-year goal on the Service Quality Indicator is to have only one tenth of the actual number of failures at the end of the fifth year that we had at the beginning of the first year, despite an annual growth of usually about 20 percent."**

"The penalty if we don't meet that goal is that no one in management—and in the higher professional ranks across the board—gets any bonus money at the end of the year," West explains. "The same applies to the service goal on the Service Quality Indicator: If we don't meet our goal, based on a six-month target, no one in management or the higher professional ranks gets any bonus money."

NOT AWARDS, BUT IMPROVEMENT IS THE PRIME OBJECTIVE

However, neither money nor awards are the primary incentives for the company's stringent quality standards: It's actually the quest for excellence that drives Federal Express to get as close as it can to 100 percent employee and customer satisfaction.

"I think it's important for people to go after the Award with self-improvement in mind," West asserts. "Many companies that call me for advice sound as if they feel that they aren't good enough to go for the Award. I think some of them are too self-critical and should give the Baldrige process a chance.

"People need to realize that they should always make *self-analysis* and *self-improvement* their goals, not winning the Award," West stresses. "They should work on meeting the criteria for the application and *then* decide whether they want to enter the application."

IBM Rochester

An entire decade devoted to strong quality initiatives led this stellar company to achieve its award winning level of excellence.

"We've always been a quality company, in our view," asserts Roy Bauer, director of Market-Driven Quality for IBM Rochester (Rochester, MN). In 1990, the Baldrige Award Committee agreed with that view—and presented one of its trophies to the site, which currently manufactures the AS/400 family of products. More than 8,100 people are responsible for developing and manufacturing these products at the Rochester facility.

"Our journey began a decade ago, when we started our formal quality initiatives," Bauer explains. "And it still continues today, even after winning the Award," says Bauer.

TAKING THE INITIATIVE FOR SUPERIOR QUALITY

Award Winning Quality

Here's a look at the stops that IBM Rochester made along the way in its decade-long journey to excellence—and the Baldrige Award:

❏ **Initiative #1: PRIDE for product reliability.** In 1981, IBM Rochester launched a set of initiatives called PRIDE (People Responsibly Involved in Developing Excellence). These initiatives focused on improving product reliability.

"We basically subscribed to Phil Crosby's zero-defects methodology," Bauer says. "We found we improved our product quality even higher than expected. Even though we thought we were good, we realized we could be a lot better."

❏ **Initiative #2: Change focus from product to process.** In 1984, the company expanded its quality emphasis by shifting its focus from product efficiency and effectiveness to *process* efficiency and effectiveness. "We implemented process manufacturing techniques through our manufacturing lines," Bauer explains. "We called this effort 'continuous flow' manufacturing or 'just-in-time' manufacturing, as it is known in the industry."

Included in process management was the need to carry out the following tasks:

➤ *identify key processes*
➤ *assign owners to the processes*
➤ *analyze the processes for efficiency, effectiveness,*

and adaptability

"This achieved some dramatic improvements in manufacturing cycle time," Bauer reports.

❏ **Initiative #3: Reduce development cycle time.** In 1986, IBM Rochester expanded its quality goals still further, with the focus shifting from making manufacturing cycle time improvements to development cycle process improvements. "We had a new laboratory director, Tom Furey, come in at that time," recalls Bauer.

"We were in the embryonic stages of starting the AS/400 project, and had been issued a challenge: Get the product out in about half the time of a normal development process. The reason was that customers were asking for new growth.

"Furey had the vision that we could do it. He felt that instead of being a little business out in the cornfields of Minnesota, we could become a major player in the computer business. This vision guided us through the next three years."

❏ **Initiative #4: Examine and apply Baldrige model.** In 1988, IBM Rochester assessed itself against the Baldrige criteria, but decided not to apply for a couple of reasons. "First, we were busy rolling out the AS/400 product," says Bauer. "Second, while we thought there were a lot of benefits to the self-assessment, we also felt that we could still make improvements in certain areas.

"We began to look at Baldrige as a model or a template that put everything we were doing into a cohesive framework. We found that we hadn't closed the loop in some of our processes, and we weren't tying our customer satisfaction feedback to our planning processes as well as we should have been."

❏ **Initiative #5: Include customers in the quality improvement process.** In 1989, IBM Rochester's quality journey extended to include market-driven customer satisfaction goals, a focus on total cycle time to market, and an increase in customer involvement.

❏ **Initiative #6: Reassess processes according to Baldrige criteria.** That same year, another self-assessment was performed, and an application was submitted to the Baldrige Committee. "We didn't win, but I also say that we didn't *lose*, because we learned more about ourselves from the assessment process," Bauer notes.

❏ **Initiative #7: Link together all elements of the organization.** In 1990, IBM Rochester positioned itself to strategically implement a new set of initiatives that linked all elements of its enterprise—development, manufacturing, marketing, and service. Incidentally, the company also won the Baldrige Award that same year.

STARTING FROM SCRATCH THE SECOND TIME

Even though IBM Rochester had already applied for the Baldrige Award in 1989, it started from scratch in 1990.

To begin with, seven senior-level executives were put on a committee that was charged with working on the application form itself. Each top manager was given ownership of one of the categories covered on the Baldrige application, which at the time were Leadership, Information and Analysis, Planning, Human Resources, Product Assurance, Quality Results, and Customer Satisfaction.

Each executive was responsible for writing his or her own portion of the application, but an in-house editor did go over their final drafts to check for clarity. Bauer also brought in several people who had been involved in previous site assessments to evaluate the drafts.

Overall, the group found that the guidelines for the self-assessment were tougher, better, and more direct in 1990 than they'd been in 1989. As they performed the self-assessment, the committee was careful to log any areas where they couldn't answer questions as "improvement items" to be worked on in 1991 and beyond.

> **"Our customers feel that IBM is _listening_ to them. They feel that they have influence in the direction we are going. We are meeting their _real_ needs, not giving them something we _think_ they need."**

SIX CRITICAL SUCCESS FACTORS BROADEN THE QUALITY PROCESS

As a result of its 1990 self-assessment IBM Rochester not only won the Baldrige Award but strategically positioned itself to implement an expanded set of initiatives built upon prior successes. The new initiatives consist of six critical success factors and proactive customer satisfaction processes.

These processes integrate all elements of development, manufacturing, marketing, and service into a market-driven quality cycle. This closed-loop cycle forms a process in which _meeting customer needs_ is the foundation.

Here's an explanation of the six key success factors:

① **Strategy:** The aim of the process is, again, to meet customer needs while supporting customer success and expanding the market.

② **Requirements:** The goal here is to establish accurate product and service specifications.

③ **Six Sigma:** These goals include reducing rework in development, manufacturing, and service areas by producing correct results the first time. (For an explanation of Six Sigma, see section on Motorola, Chapter Two, Figure 2-1.)

④ **Employee Education:** This involves teaching people how they can better understand the need to change the company's culture, and empowering them to play an active role in that change.

⑤ **Employee Involvement:** These goals focus on increasing participation and productivity.

⑥ **Cycle time Reduction:** Here, the company is trying to ensure faster market response and develop an increased competitive advantage.

CUSTOMERS AND PLANNING HELP IBM ROCHESTER BECOME A LEADER

Contributing to IBM Rochester's Baldrige win is the fact that it is a clear leader in two areas considered important by the Award examiners. These areas involve _customer satisfaction_ and _planning_:

➪ **Customer satisfaction.** IBM Rochester sets up customer councils, in which the company actually reviews one- to two-year plans with its customers in advance. If customers don't like the plans, the plans are changed.

"The power of this concept is that our customers feel that IBM is _listening_ to them," says Bauer. "They feel that they have influence in the direction we are going. We are meeting their _real_ needs, not giving them something we _think_ they need.

"I believe that the Baldrige people would say that we are industry leaders in involving our customers in our plans and development activities."

➪ **Planning.** This is another area in which IBM

Rochester has become a leader. "We have about 450,000 Systems 3X and AS/400 in our installed base, and over 60 percent of that is in locations other than the United States," Bauer estimates. "We have developed a consistent methodology that makes us an industry leader in market segmentation."

This is important in terms of the Award, he notes, because the Baldrige examiners look at how you plan and whether you understand the market you are in at the present time, as well as the markets you wish to enter in the future.

Bauer adds that the Baldrige people also ask the following customer- and planning-related questions:

❖ *How do you balance customer satisfaction with business growth?*

❖ *How do you know the requirements you're using are the ones customers want?*

❖ *Is your planning process definable, repeatable, and predictable?*

"There are not many planning processes that have these characteristics—but these are the characteristics of *our* planning system," says Bauer.

THE AWARD COMES SECOND; SELF-ASSESSMENT COMES FIRST

Bauer is quick to emphasize that you shouldn't build up your quality program just in hopes of winning the trophy itself. "People need to think of applying for the Baldrige Award as secondary. The benefits you get from doing the self-assessment are what *really* count," he stresses.

> **You shouldn't build up your quality program just in hopes of winning the trophy itself. "People need to think of applying for the Baldrige Award as secondary. The benefits you get from doing the self-assessment are what <u>really</u> count."**

"We were good before Baldrige came along, but we are going to be a lot better because of it," Bauer continues. "The reason for this is that we're working on problems and opportunities we didn't even know about until we got into self-assessment. The questions cause you to think about how you do things in your company."

Of course, actually winning the Award has its benefits, too. "Winning the Baldrige Award affirms to me that the path we've been on the past ten years is the correct one," says Bauer. "It has helped us be more specific about what we want in the future and what we need to do to get better. I believe that this knowledge is going to propel IBM Rochester ahead in the future."

The Wallace Company, Inc.

A comprehensive seven-step plan helped this company to make a quality turnaround in record time—and then capture a Baldrige Award to boot.

The Wallace Co., Inc. (Houston, TX), founded in 1942, is an industrial distributor of pipes, valves, fittings, and other products for chemical and petrochemical plants. In the mid-1980s, the 200-employee company was watching its competitors go bankrupt while its own primary source of revenue was drying up. Oil prices plummeted and the petroleum industry toppled into one of the worst slumps in recent history. What had once been a booming economic climate went *bust*.

However, instead of throwing in the towel in the face of this less-than-rosy scenario, Wallace resolved to make a turnaround.

"Our search for quality improvement was necessary for our company's survival," says Plant Operations Manager Trudy Kurz. "When things got really tough in the oil industry, we knew that short-term remedies would not solve our problems—so we decided to concentrate on long-term quality improvement, with a strong emphasis on customer service and employee training," she explains.

Wallace made its commitment to quality in 1985, when Hoescht-Celanese, one of its major customers, informed the company that it wanted to limit its supplier base to only those suppliers that could demonstrate reliable quality. This meant giving Hoescht-Celanese *what it wanted, when it wanted it, every time*. "They told us that if we didn't get involved in a quality improvement process, we would lose their account," says Kurz.

"We realized that to be able to give our customers what they demanded—accurate and complete shipments, on-time delivery performance, and error-free transactions—we would have to make a companywide commitment to the overall quality process.

"This led to our first program, which consisted of quality circles, and I was part of the very first one," she recalls. "However, we weren't entirely ready for it. Since management really didn't know what it wanted us to do, we didn't know what we were *supposed* to do. The upshot was, the biggest innovation that our circles came up with was the creation of an Employee of the Month program. And that really had nothing to do with quality.

"So we continued our search for quality. In 1987, we began making the changes that ultimately led to our winning the Baldrige Award."

Let's take a close look at the strategy that helped Wallace beat the odds and become a winner.

OVERCOMING EARLY OBSTACLES: NEEDS ASSESSMENT HELPS PINPOINT PROBLEMS

The first steps on the quality journey were difficult, mostly because the company's quality efforts really didn't have much direction. After trying quality circles without getting the changes it wanted, the company hired a corporate training firm to carry out a needs assessment.

Before beginning the assessment, the training firm asked the management team if it would be receptive to the results—*no matter what*. "We had to do some soul-searching, but we agreed," recalls John Wallace, the company's CEO. Indeed, some problems were soon uncovered.

"This firm met individually with every associate in our company and asked each of them what he or she considered to be the weaknesses in our operation," says Kurz (at Wallace, employees are called "associates"). "They assured the associates that everything they said would be held in strict confidence.

"Based on its findings, the firm's report indicated that we needed better communication, more training, and a more open and positive atmo-

Award Winning Quality

> **"When things got really tough in the oil industry, we knew that short-term remedies would not solve our problems—so we decided to concentrate on long-term quality improvement, with a strong emphasis on customer service and employee training."**

sphere." The needs assessment indicated that there was a significant amount of fear that was impeding communications in the organization. The report also stated that there was a need for effective on-the-job training and cross-training. "We had enough training to realize that until we got rid of the fear factor, we wouldn't be successful," says CEO John Wallace. "Because we are family owned, we thought we had one big family. We found out that we *didn't*."

"We then retained consultants who helped us develop a quality program," says Kurz. "They gave us training in various quality procedures and helped us put together quality improvement process teams." To help overcome the fear factor, key executives attended every training session given at all 10 company sites. The idea was for the employees and top management to get to know one another, to share and solve problems, and to become comfortable communicating with one another.

"We held seminars at hotels on Saturdays where everybody—from the people who sweep our floors to CEO John Wallace—attended and participated in team meetings. These seminars probably provided our biggest breakthrough," Kurz recalls. "At first, most of the associates attending the seminars were too intimidated to say anything while upper management was in the room.

"However, as people began to see that this program was for real—and that all of management was behind it—the atmosphere started changing. The intimidation and fear was replaced by a camaraderie; a trust and fellowship developed throughout the entire organization. No one left those seminars untouched."

As the culture changed, employees finally started coming to top management with their problems and suggestions.

THE BALDRIGE PROCESS HELPS INSPIRE FURTHER IMPROVEMENTS

The quality improvement process got another boost in 1989. The Wallace Company got a flyer in the mail from the National Institute of Standards and Technology regarding a Quest for Excellence conference in Washington, D.C. Two Wallace staffers decided to go, and while there, they heard the story of how Motorola, Globe Metallurgical, and Commercial Nuclear Fuel Division of Westinghouse (see Chapter Two) had won their Baldrige Awards.

The conference attendees from Wallace struck up a friendship with Ken Leach, vice president of Globe Metallurgical (which is about the same size as Wallace). Leach gave them encouragement to go after the Award. However, they came back with the sense that the company wasn't as far along as everyone hoped it was.

People at Wallace realized that the company needed to do a lot of work to catch up with the level of excellence achieved by the previous winners. A decision was made to take the Baldrige criteria and use them as the guide for Wallace's quality quest.

TAKING SEVEN GIANT STEPS TOWARD QUALITY SUCCESS

At that time, the Baldrige Award required applicants to demonstrate their excellence in seven categories: Leadership, Information and Analysis, Strategic Quality Planning, Human Resource Utilization, Quality Assurance of Products and Services, Quality Results, and Customer Satisfaction (some changes have been made to the criteria; see Chapter One).

Wallace took these seven areas and graded itself rather harshly against the criteria in each. When areas for improvement were found, Wallace staffers began to develop strategies for making improvements in those areas.

> "What employees now realize is that whenever you have to sign your name to a job, you're going to take more pride in what you do...you're going to make sure the job is done right. We were trying to get employees to take <u>ownership</u> of their work, and we've succeeded."

Here's what Wallace did in each of the seven significant areas:

❑ **Leadership.** This category examines whether leaders of a company can create and sustain a value system and a supporting management system that will guide the company to achieve quality excellence. It also evaluates whether the company reaches out to the community in leadership roles consistent with its internal quality values and practices.

The commitment was made at Wallace that the quality improvement efforts would be led by a Quality Management Steering Committee composed of the

CEO, the president, the vice president, the executive vice president, and the vice president-Finance. The members interact informally daily because the company is small, but they hold a formal meeting once a month.

In addition, each member of this group attended over 200 hours of training in Continuous Quality Improvement, since each training session of associates is either taught or attended by a senior-level executive.

Senior-level executives and managers also serve on key teams that formulate the quality improvement process, and on interdepartmental teams, where they bring internal customers and suppliers together to solve problems.

❑ **Information and Analysis.** This category examines the scope, validity, use, and management of data and information that are the foundation of the organization's quality management system. Wallace used three criteria to determine the types of quality-related data it would maintain in its information base:

○ *Did the data meet internal customers' needs?* This included sales reports, inventory records, and financial statements from the company's 10 branches.

○ *Did the data meet external customers' needs*, such as on-time delivery to the right place?

○ *Did the data help improve the company's quality leadership practices?* This included increased employee satisfaction leading to low turnover, as well as reduced absenteeism and tardiness.

The Quality Management Steering Committee reviews data monthly to plan short- and long-range goals, while trying to spot specific areas that need improvement.

❑ **Strategic Quality Planning.** This category covers the company's planning process for retaining or achieving quality leadership, the integration of quality improvement planning into the overall business plan, and the short- and long-term priorities to achieve or sustain a quality leadership position.

At Wallace, 16 Quality Strategic Objectives drive the process of quality improvement:

⇨ *Leadership development*
⇨ *Quality business plan*
⇨ *On-the-job training*
⇨ *Information analysis*
⇨ *Statistical process control*
⇨ *Quality education*
⇨ *Human resource development*
⇨ *Quality improvement process team involvement*

⇨ *Customer service/satisfaction*
⇨ *Employee reinforcement/incentive*
⇨ *Quality pathfinder*
⇨ *Suggestion system*
⇨ *Internal audit*
⇨ *Internal and external benchmarking*
⇨ *Vendor quality improvement plan*
⇨ *Community outreach*

The main types of data analyzed are customer focused, because Wallace's planning is customer focused. Each month, the Steering Committee assesses customer and market analysis reports, trends in customer complaints, and changes in customer specifications or audit criteria.

Both associates and suppliers participate in the revision of the quality business plan. As a result of this process, Wallace has significantly reduced its supplier base. And those suppliers that remain are quite responsive: Through Wallace's vendor certification process, the company can monitor its customers' needs and then obtain the necessary improvements from its vendors as customers' requirements change.

❑ **Human Resource Utilization.** The effectiveness of the company's efforts to develop the full potential of its work force and to maintain an environment conducive to teamwork, quality leadership, and personal growth is measured in this category.

As part of its Quality Strategic Objectives, Wallace established both short- and long-term goals. Short-term goals included responding to new suggestions within one day, increasing skills such as coaching, and developing new employee assistance and community outreach programs. Long-term goals included setting the industry standard for safety, starting a management intern program, and strong career/education development for associates.

Specifically, associates receive training that is targeted to develop skills in quality awareness, customer service, problem-solving, communication skills, and mastery of materials, skills, and new tools needed for their jobs. They may also volunteer for teams that meet weekly, usually during working hours, to solve problems, streamline job processes, and improve cycle time reduction as well as processes in all divisions.

Associates are rewarded for participation on teams and in training through articles recognizing their accomplishments in the company newsletter, congratulatory letters from the CEO, picnics, and dinners. In the face of this increased responsibility and recognition, Wallace has seen its absenteeism rate fall to less than half the industry average, while turnover has declined to less than three percent.

❑ **Quality Assurance of Products and Services.** This category examines the systematic approaches used by the company for total quality assurance of goods and services. Continuous quality improvement and how it is applied across the organization is assessed in this section.

For example, Wallace found that the two quality characteristics consistently identified as most important by its customers were *complete, on-time delivery* and *accurate invoicing*. Customer profiling of each account contains information unique to each, and is available to all associates. On-time delivery and accuracy of invoices are charted because they are considered to be areas that need *constant* improvement. Associate teams are continuously reviewing processes, and any improvements are put on-line to be shared by all branches.

❑ **Quality Results.** This category examines quality levels and improvements based upon objective measures. These figures come from analyses of customer requirements and expectations as well as from analyses of business operations. These are compared with quality levels in competing firms.

As a result of its improvement efforts, Wallace found that its on-time delivery rate had risen from 75 percent in 1987 to 92 percent in 1990, while the industry average was 86.3 percent. In addition, on-time delivery to "partnering" customers rose to 97 percent, due in large part to having a continuous dialogue with these customers.

Other reports revealed the following information:

➤ *Sales for 1985 to 1989 increased by 40 percent, while inventory was reduced by 5 percent.*

➤ *Inventory turns improved by 175 percent in 5 years, and are currently 27 percent better than the industry average.*

➤ *Average number of days for outstanding accounts receivable in 1986 to 1989 were reduced by 11 days, resulting in substantial savings in interest.*

❑ **Customer Satisfaction.** This area examines knowledge of the customer, service systems, responsiveness, and ability to meet requirements and expectations. To gain this knowledge, Wallace gets feedback from its outside salespeople as well as from customer surveys. Four types of surveys are used:

① *A semiannual survey that asks customers to evaluate existing services*

② *An annual "blind" survey done by an outside service to gather similar information, as well as competitor information*

③ *One-minute surveys to assess requirements of a*

specific individual or account

④ *A post card survey that is attached to every outbound shipment to get customer comments*

"We've also started a companywide program called 'The Total Customer Involvement Program,'" notes Kurz. "The goal of this program is to have every associate in our company visit a customer at least one day every year.

"For example, someone from our accounts receivable department will go to a customer's accounts payable department. They'll sit and discuss procedures, types of problems they've encountered, and so on." When employees are able to "walk a mile" in their customers' shoes, their quality awareness is enhanced dramatically—and with it, their willingness to assure that they do every job right the first time.

The company has also developed other programs, procedures, and techniques (including extended warranties and the handling of complaints by well-trained people) that meet or exceed the industry standards for maintaining customer satisfaction.

Here are two of these techniques in action:

➤ **Holding employees accountable.** "After our order fillers finish with an order, they must now sign the customer sales order slip," Kurz explains. "In fact, we've got a brief statement on the sales order that reads, '*This sales order has been filled and checked in accordance with customer requirements and is accurate to the best of my knowledge.*' We ask our truck drivers to sign the sales order slips as well.

"Initially, people balked at having to sign these slips. They thought that we were just using this procedure so that we could point the finger at them if they made a mistake. What we were trying to achieve, however, and what employees now realize, is that whenever you have to sign your name to a job, you're going to put forth some extra effort and take a lot more pride in what you do. When your name is on it, you're going to make sure the job is done right. We were trying to get employees to take *ownership* of their work, and we've succeeded with that."

➤ **Assigning specific accounts.** "Instead of having our order fillers just take any order that happens to come in, we've assigned specific accounts to each of them," Kurz says. "So in essence, their accounts are their customers. The order fillers make on-site visits to the receiving departments of the accounts they are in charge of. This step has proven to be very beneficial."

How satisfied *are* Wallace's customers? Consider these statistics:

★ In 1989, Wallace set an all-time record by scoring

97.97 on a Monsanto audit.

★ Wallace is Lubrizol's top-rated supplier, with a performance rating of 98 percent or better.

★ Wallace outperformed all other suppliers to Dow Chemical USA Freeport with an on-time delivery rating of 98.4.

In addition, customer complaints have dropped dramatically.

TEAMWORK FACILITATES PROBLEM-SOLVING AND QUALITY IMPROVEMENT

According to Kurz, one of the biggest changes Wallace's quality improvement effort has brought about is the major role teams now play in the organization. "I would estimate that more than 80 percent of the day-to-day decisions made here now are done through the team process," she explains.

"Besides participating in their natural work teams, most associates also belong to other teams. Whenever an associate comes to me with a work-related problem, I make that person a team leader and direct him or her to put together a team to study the problem."

> "You can't simply place people on teams and expect the outcome to be favorable. In order to achieve success, you need to create an atmosphere that is conducive to teamwork and establish some guidelines."

"At first, I think people were afraid to approach me with problems because they knew I would make them a team leader," she notes. "But once they began to see things around them improving, they realized that by working together as a team, they could make some positive changes in their workplace. Consequently, now many of our people are on two or three teams.

"However, you can't simply place people on teams and expect the outcome to be favorable," warns Kurz. "In order to achieve success, you need to create an atmosphere that is conducive to teamwork and establish some guidelines. One of our primary rules is that a team member is not allowed to tell a fellow teammate that his or her idea is 'stupid' or that it 'doesn't make sense.'

"Whenever someone comes up with an idea—no matter how crazy or off-the-wall it may seem—it should be discussed," she stresses. "After all, you never know what will come of it or what other ideas it may generate. And that's the kind of free-thinking atmosphere that encourages people to contribute."

QUALITY IMPROVEMENTS ABOUND AT THE WALLACE COMPANY

"When you have an entire organization working together toward a common goal, the results can be phenomenal," Kurz emphasizes. Some of these results at Wallace include the following:

★ **A clean and well-organized workplace.** "Our safety committee saw to it that all pallets were removed from the aisles," she explains. "A couple of other teams tackled the job of reorganizing the warehouse and getting things laid out better.

"It's obvious that our associates take a lot more pride in their workplace than they did before. People have even taken it upon themselves to sweep the warehouse every day! They're always cleaning up the facility."

★ **Improved on-time delivery.** "Our on-time delivery rose from 75 percent in 1987 to over 92 percent presently," Kurz reports. This is well above the industry average of 86.3 percent. "And the kicker is that we accomplished this while carrying less inventory!

"We used to stock $30-$40 million worth of inventory companywide, but now we're down to about $17 million. We started buying smarter and stopped stocking as many 'nuisance' items. By nuisance items, I mean the small items that we sell a lot of. We actually found that we can get these at just as good a price if we buy them when needed than if we purchased them in quantity and stocked them. In addition, we trimmed our number of suppliers from 3,000 down to fewer than 300."

★ **A better safety record.** "Safety was one area that received a lot of our attention," notes Kurz. "Previously, safety was focused upon only as a reaction to accidents or problems. But now we try to eliminate problems before they occur. Our workers are empowered to stop an operation at any time to remove a safety hazard.

"Since instituting our safety program, we've had a dramatic reduction in the number of injuries. Furthermore, we reduced insurance costs by $500,000 in one year as a direct result of our safety program."

★ **Effective training programs in place.** "Our

company has invested about $2 million in formal training since 1987," says Kurz. "Everyone receives quality awareness training. Our other training programs focus on such topics as leadership, coaching, cycle time reduction, communication, statistical process control, data collection skills, and product knowledge.

"We also started training and certifying programs for operators of our forklifts, order-picking equipment, pettibones, and cranes."

★ **Substantially improved morale.** "Since 1987, absenteeism has fallen from 1.4 percent to .7 percent, which is less than half the industry average," notes Kurz. "And turnover has declined from about 7 percent to under 3 percent."

SOME FINAL WORDS OF ADVICE:
SET GOALS, THEN LEARN FROM THE BEST

If your company chooses to use consultants to assist with setting up a quality improvement program, it shouldn't "put all its eggs in one basket," Kurz advises. "You shouldn't expect one consultant to come in and do everything for you and handle all your departments. You need to retain consultants who specialize in certain areas.

"However, before you even bring consultants into the picture, you need to *identify some of your company's problems* and *establish a goal*. If you try to just go in and start a quality program without a goal, you're going to be lost. You need to have some idea of what you want to accomplish."

Kurz says a good place to turn for help with setting goals is the application for the Baldrige Award. "Study the requirements for that program," she suggests. "Another good source of information is ISO (International Standards Organization) certification material, which gives you international quality standards." The Wallace Company was ISO certified in 1991. By looking at the standards set by the Baldrige Award and ISO, you'll see the areas on which your company needs to concentrate its quality efforts.

"We learned some valuable lessons by studying the requirements of these organizations," Kurz reports.

> **"If you try to just go in and start a quality program without a goal, you're going to be lost. You need to have some idea of what you want to accomplish."**

Although her company relied on the advice of consultants, Kurz believes that today you can succeed without the services of these professionals. "There are so many companies with quality programs now that you can benchmark instead." (By benchmarking she means analyzing and learning from the successful processes that are in place at other companies.) "These companies have already acquired the knowledge, they've been through the training, and they've used consultants," she explains.

"We went to other companies to see what their computer systems were like, how they delivered material, what they did about training, how they handled safety, and so on. This is a fantastic way to learn first-hand what works and what doesn't.

"Once you have a successful quality program in place, don't be surprised when people from other companies want to come and see how *your* program works," Kurz adds. "Since winning the Baldrige Award, we've been so inundated with requests to look at our operation that we've had to schedule a regular Visitors' Day!"

Chapter Five

Malcolm Baldrige National Quality Award Winners—1991

Marlow Industries

Although this already excellent company certainly didn't *need* "fixing," it made its manufacturing and service operations even better through Total Quality Management—and won a Baldrige Award in recognition of its efforts.

"We have always envisioned ourselves as a quality company," asserts Raymond Marlow, president and CEO of Marlow Industries (Dallas). "We are a high-tech business with a custom-designed product for our customers. Sixty percent of our customers are military and aerospace."

Marlow Industries manufactures customized thermoelectric (TE) cooling modules that heat, cool, or stabilize the temperature of electronic equipment. From its founding in 1973, the company has quickly grown from a five-person operation to a staff of 160 in 1991, and it has increased its share of the world's market for TE coolers to more than 50 percent. As of this writing, Marlow Industries has total annual sales of $12 million, with exports accounting for 15 percent of its annual sales.

Since 1987, the company has increased its productivity 10 percent *each year* and has cut its cost of scrap, rework, and other nonconformance errors by nearly 50 percent. Every gain Marlow Industries has achieved has been translated into benefits for its customers. These benefits include products that exceed performance specifications by wide margins; consistent on-time deliveries; extended warranties; and prices that have remained stable—or *decreased*.

With so much to offer its customers, it's no wonder that Marlow Industries has been so successful and that it merited the Malcolm Baldrige National Quality Award—in the small business category—in 1991.

Below, Raymond Marlow and Chief Operating Officer Christian Witzke explain how the company used an evolving system of continuous improvement through Total Quality Management to attain its current level of excellence. They also share the steps they followed to apply for the Baldrige Award.

TAKING THE FIRST STEPS TOWARD TOTAL QUALITY

Marlow reports that when he first sought to instill a quality process at the company, he initially decided to go directly to the employees and tell them about what he felt a quality system was. However, "after three months of talking about our quality system to the hourly employees once a week, an hour at a time, I found that my approach wasn't working," he concedes.

The problem was that the hourly employees didn't understand why the president of the company was talking to them about quality. They believed that the quality effort was something the company was going to do for a while, and then it would fizzle out.

Another source of resistance came from managers: They didn't like the fact that Marlow was bypassing them and going directly to the hourly employees. "What this told me is that you can't implement a quality process from the bottom up. You have to do it from the top down," says Marlow.

As Marlow was learning this first lesson about quality system implementation, a challenge to improve came from the company's customers. "Around 1985, our customers began to tell us what quality they wanted in the products we produced for them," he reports.

"We knew we needed to start some type of formal quality program that went from the top down. That's when we participated in the formation of—and subsequently joined—the first group of the Texas Quality Consortium, which was a group of small businesses in the Dallas area that were interested in learning more about quality.

"As a member of the consortium, we learned about quality awareness: what it was, and the importance of having all levels of management as well as hourly employees involved in a quality process."

Award Winning Quality

> **"We learned about quality awareness: what it was, and the importance of having all levels of management as well as hourly employees involved in a quality process."**

"We continued to grow in our quality knowledge for the next two years," Marlow continues. "Basically what we did was to go through Crosby, Deming, Juran, quality awareness, and right on through the steps required to establish a Total Quality Management system."

BALDRIGE APPLICATION PROVIDES BLUEPRINT FOR TOTAL QUALITY

Marlow Industries had the awareness and desire to formulate a continuous improvement process in-house, but its effort was not yet structured. Then the Baldrige application was born, and it provided the quality blueprint that Marlow was seeking.

"When the Baldrige application came out in 1988, we looked at it and felt that this was potentially what we were looking for," Marlow says. "At that time, we weren't looking for an award, but more for a quality system that was based on continuous improvement as the method of achieving customer satisfaction.

"We liked the Baldrige criteria because they were built around customer satisfaction and encompass all aspects of the business." And those are the driving principles behind Total Quality Management, suggests Marlow.

Chief Operating Officer Christian Witzke agrees: "That's right—our original intent was not to win the Award. Basically, we just wanted to continuously improve.

"We knew about ever-increasing customer quality standards," Witzke continues. "We were doing pretty well with customers as far as our worldwide market share was concerned. For example, we were doing business with Japan and with the aerospace industry. They were long-term customers that had been with us more than 10 years; we had never lost a major customer.

"We knew we were doing some things right, but we felt that we needed to improve overall, on a wider scope," Witzke adds. "We believed that if we would compete for the Baldrige Award, we could use the critiquing as a benchmark to improve our world-class image."

QUALITY COUNCIL FORMED TO ADDRESS BALDRIGE APPLICATION

"We looked at the 1988, '89, and '90 Baldrige applications," Marlow reports. "In 1990, we decided to apply for the Baldrige Award. We wrote a couple of drafts for the application, but it wasn't until 1991 that we really went after the Award.

"We felt that winning the Award would be great, but we were just as interested in the critiquing we would receive as a result of submitting our application. And if we were lucky enough to get a site visit, we would get even more critiquing. We felt that the feedback the examiners would provide would help us on the course we wanted, which was to establish a structured, continuous improvement program throughout all our business operations over the years.

"I think the changes in the application from 1988 to the present time have made it tougher," Marlow adds. "My earlier experiences in trying to inform employees about quality on my own, as well as the years we were participants in the Texas Quality Consortium, were very helpful to us when we started to fill out the Baldrige application.

"Without those earlier experiences, we would not have been ready to tackle the Baldrige application. The Baldrige application is like going to 'graduate school.' First, you should learn about quality awareness in an activity such as the Texas Quality Consortium, which is more like 'high school.' By the time we got to the Baldrige application, we had been into our quality awareness program about two and one-half years," says Marlow.

> "We felt that the feedback the examiners would provide would help us on the course we wanted, which was to establish a structured, continuous improvement program throughout all our business operations over the years."

"We already had a quality policy, a pledge, a strategic vision—those types of items," Witzke points out. "The next thing we worked on was how to get these items implemented. We had a quality council consisting of the president, vice presidents, senior managers, and some staff members. Both Crosby and Deming include, as one of their steps, putting together a council to oversee the quality system."

Starting a quality council was not without its problems, however: Soon after the council got started, it began to run into problems. "If you are not careful when you are forming your council, you may find that you have created a separate structure from your organizational structure for managing your quality program," Marlow warns.

"For instance, there was a committee that was looking at improving a particular area. Our original quality council got frustrated after a length of time. They were not able to make any changes happen because they were not a part of the management chain of command. The way you make changes happen is by going through the chain of command.

"We found that our quality council had to be a part

of our management structure and that it had to be responsible not only for quality but also for profits," Marlow stresses.

THE TOTAL QUALITY MANAGEMENT COUNCIL IS FORMED

"We reorganized the Quality Council and changed its name to the 'Total Quality Management Council' (TQC)," explains Witzke. "We decided that would be an overseeing board—like a board of advisors. Management was on the council. The council was not responsible for implementation. It was only responsible for overseeing the system and identifying weaknesses, gaps, etc.

"Once the council identifies a problem, management assumes responsibility for setting goals and coming up with solutions to the problem. For example, if there is a problem getting an accurate measure of customer satisfaction, the council might recommend that the marketing vice president or manager work on establishing such a measurement."

Top management now had to give the department managers the necessary tools to do the follow-up on any requests from the TQC. "We organized the manufacturing areas so that the resources were there to manage requests from the TQC," says Witzke. "We integrated the support organizations into the line organization, such as marketing. Each level in the chain of command then assumed its share of the responsibility for coming up with solutions to problems and implementing the solutions."

The TQC defines the company's biggest problems. Then they assign resources from different areas in the company and put people on a team to solve those problems.

GETTING EVERYONE ON THE QUALITY FORCE

Part of every successful TQM effort is getting everyone at the company involved in the total quality process. Here are the steps followed at Marlow Industries to assure total quality awareness and training throughout the organization:

✪ **Have top management set the "quality awareness" example.** As the president and CEO, Raymond Marlow is recognized as the leader of the quality program. He and the upper level managers at the company are aware of their responsibilities to act as role models for their continuous quality awareness process.

To do this, these managers all make quality awareness a part of their everyday communication with employees at all levels. They sponsor many company events to give recognition to teams and individuals who make outstanding contributions to their quality process.

✪ **Train from the top down.** "We already had our people *aware* of quality and the need for continuous improvement," says Witzke. "Now, they needed to know *what to do.*

"We started out by training management," he continues. "Texas Instruments helped us by allowing us to use its team training program to train our supervisors and employees." (Both Marlow and Witzke are former Texas Instruments staff members. See Chapter Six for a look at TI's Baldrige-influenced quality system.) "Of course, we had to adapt the programs somewhat to meet Marlow Industries' needs and culture.

"After the supervisors were trained, they became the planners, implementers, and trainers of their employees."

✪ **Start a job certification training program.** After the managers were trained, they started to think about training for their employees. At first, the TQM council and management created technical training programs in such subjects as statistical process control and the skills needed to operate various machines, using outside courses where possible. However, they eventually decided that they would be better off having their own managers do the training.

At that stage, they put together a job certification training program. To do this, the employees and supervisors first revised and updated the procedures needed to carry out each job. Then they developed a hands-on application test and a written examination. Employees who passed these tests received certification. The supervisors also had to go through the same tests so that they understood what their employees were learning.

As a result of the certification program, employees now understand the technical side of their jobs so well that if something breaks down, they can usually fix it themselves.

THREE TYPES OF EMPLOYEE TEAMS HELP DEEPEN TOTAL QUALITY INVOLVEMENT

In 1988, 44 percent of all personnel at Marlow Industries were active on teams. However, by 1990, this number had doubled: 88 percent of all personnel were involved in teams. Here is a look at each of the types of employee teams that have been deployed at the company:

① **Corporate Action Teams.** The first type of team is the corporate action team (CAT). These teams focus on solving corporate-level goals. They concentrate on critical problems and needs that involve more than one department and that are cross-functional in nature. Team members are picked by the TQM council for their skills and are placed on these teams. CATs have no volunteers. At the completion of the task, these teams disband.

② **Employee Effectiveness Teams.** The second type of team, employee effectiveness teams, focuses on *preventing* potential problems in specific work areas. Members of these teams are volunteers, usually from their local work areas. They pick their own problems to work on without direction from management. Department managers and supervisors instruct them in team training and problem-solving skills. This gives the managers and supervisors a hand in the process, and they know what their teams are doing.

The employee effectiveness teams start out by brainstorming a list of problems. Then they decide which problem to work on first. However, Marlow states, "as they were looking through their first problem, they saw other problems on their list that they realized they could immediately fix.

"It turned out that they solved half their list by just deciding not to do something anymore, or just to do it in a different way. In effect, they solved one official problem, but in the course of doing that, they solved a lot of little problems very quickly. That gave them a sense of accomplishment and empowerment. The supervisors saw that and didn't feel so threatened after all by empowering their people."

③ **Department Action Teams.** "The department action team (DAT) is the team in the middle," Marlow explains. "The department manager can set this up to solve problems in a department. The managers can go outside their departments for technical assistance if they need some help, for example, in drafting or quality assurance.

"For example, customer service and marketing people might work together to decide how to respond to customer complaints faster. The department works on a *directed* problem rather than a volunteer problem."

Marlow Industries uses three specific factors to keep the quality teams motivated to helping the company achieve excellence in all its endeavors:

➤ *Recognition for problem-solving:* When a team solves a problem, it makes a presentation to the Total Quality council. This is a form of management recognition. The teams are then recognized for their quality contributions in the monthly company meetings, which all employees attend.

➤ *Team champions:* "Another thing that we think has helped the team concept is that each team has a champion," Marlow points out. "The champion is responsible for leading the team, keeping the minutes [at team meetings], and for making things happen.

"With the employee teams, we picked the champions at the start because we wanted people who had been through the team leadership course. Later on, the teams could pick their own champions."

➤ *Team mentors:* "Each team also has a mentor," says Witzke. "Mentors are from senior management or from the Total Quality Management Council, and they are assigned to the teams. I am a mentor to five teams.

"The mentor's job is to go to the team meetings, but not to be the champion. The mentor is only there to break down any barriers that the team runs into—for instance, to help if they need money, resources, or assistance from other departments. So the mentor sits quietly and watches how the process works. You are auditing the *process* rather than the problem.

"A hidden advantage is that the Total Quality Management council and management both have a direct connection with the team activities, so they don't have to formally review the teams' status all the time," says Witzke.

TEAMWORK WITH CUSTOMERS AND SUPPLIERS: FORMING CRITICAL QUALITY PARTNERSHIPS

In addition to total involvement of all personnel *within* the company, another factor that has helped Marlow Industries grow its total quality process is the involvement of some people *outside* the company: customers and suppliers. Top management at the company has formed close working relationships with both customers and suppliers.

First, managers developed positive working relationships with their largest suppliers. Then, they used the knowledge they gained from working with them to develop partnerships with their customers. Marlow explains how the company did this: "First, we listed all our suppliers. Then we took the top 20 percent, which represents about 80 percent of our purchases.

"Next, we worked up a Marlow Supplier Quality Index, which looked at the quality of the product they delivered, their on-time delivery, and other pertinent information, and we shared our findings with them. This gave them the feedback that told them whether they are or are not meeting our expectations.

"We also told them that our new philosophy was to minimize the number of suppliers that we have and to develop a very close working relationship with those remaining suppliers in the future," Marlow points out.

"When we start developing new product designs, which we do continuously, the suppliers are a part of the design team," he continues. "That means our suppliers are involved in the process almost as soon as our product design engineers are. They know that if the new program is successful, they are going to get the program, so they are willing to do a little extra—

whether it's making a prototype or giving technical assistance."

"As a small business, we are somewhat limited in resources and development of additional skills," says Witzke. "So the advantage of having a close relationship with a few suppliers is that if we need special skills, such as ceramics, instead of establishing a ceramics engineer in-house, we depend on our ceramic suppliers to furnish technology and those skills to us. We get leverage from their technical skills, and since that's their primary business focus, they know more about ceramics than we will ever know. We can tap that knowledge.

> **"We may put money into research and development up front for our customers because we feel that it is a lot easier and cheaper to keep customers than it is to gain them back after you have lost them. You might as well spend your money _wisely_."**

"The suppliers benefit by getting our business without competing with our in-house capability," Witzke adds. "We've been successful getting that kind of support from our top 20 suppliers. Because of our close working relationship, we are expecting that we will soon accept work from our top 20 suppliers without inspection."

Marlow Industries also works very closely with its customers. "When we develop a working relationship with a customer, we feel that we can put expenditures and funds into something that supports them," Marlow asserts. "Normally, a lot of companies would not do this; but we are comfortable that if _we_ do it, our customers will give us the order.

"Over 90 percent of our products are custom-designed to meet a customer's specific needs," Marlow continues. "We do not sell through representatives, distributors, or field sales personnel in the United States. We have a sales and marketing group here in Dallas. This group is basically made up of engineering

people in our marketing department. They initiate the programs with our customers, and once we get the order, one to three engineers are assigned to the customer's program. They keep in touch with the customer on almost a daily basis to make sure we know what they are doing and that they know exactly what we are doing."

"Our strategic plan is to focus more on developing long-term customer relationships than on selling our products," Witzke notes. "We like to sell products, but we believe this happens more easily after the relationships have been built.

"As an example, we may put money into research and development up front for our customers because we feel that it is a lot easier and cheaper to keep customers than it is to gain them back after you have lost them. You might as well spend your money _wisely_.

"If a customer comes back with a problem such as damaged products, we just take them back without any fuss because we desire to create a long-term relationship." Witzke adds that Marlow Industries has more than reaped the benefits of that cooperative attitude toward its customers.

WRITING THE BALDRIGE APPLICATION: SOME TIPS FOR SUCCESS

With its Total Quality process well in place, Marlow Industries took a highly methodical approach to applying for the Award. Its preparation began two years before it actually won.

Here are the steps that helped lead the company to its ultimate success:

★ **Form a Baldrige team.** In 1989, the Total Quality Management council initially formed a Baldrige Action Team (BAT). They initially divided the application between seven different teams, and like the other teams described above, each team had a champion and a mentor. There were six people on each team.

"The teams self-audited us against the Baldrige application and developed a list of recommended improvements," Marlow explains. "When we actually drafted the application in 1990, we formed a seven-person BAT champion team (composed mostly of senior management) to write it."

★ **Define terms on the application to assure complete comprehension.** Each champion drafted his or her section of the application, and then the other champions reviewed one another's sections. This led to problems because each champion was using different definitions of words found in the application questions.

They also found that they were not familiar with the intent of some of the words in the application. Thus, their next step was to come up with a list of definitions that all groups could use.

★ **Exchange and review drafts.** "We first began writing the application over a period of 18 months," says Witzke. "However, when we got serious about applying, we wrote the final application in February or March. We did several drafts and circulated them, and another team would grade that draft. After they pointed out weaknesses that needed fixing, they would look at the next draft. We got down to fewer people as we went along."

★ **Edit the drafts *carefully*.** "We allocated each of the pages on the basis of a point system," Witzke explains. "Our president and CEO had 'leadership,' which was supposed to be nine pages long. He had 23 pages on his first draft."

"I was determined to cover everything," says Marlow. "What you find out is that in shortening, you lose some of it. It's not like a novel. You might have a sentence that doesn't seem to have anything to do with the paragraph above or below it, but it answered a specific item that they asked for in the application, in the sequence in which they asked for it. So you have to be very careful when you start going back over your work to edit it."

> "Every year, the competition gets stiffer, and your customers' requirements increase. Therefore, every year, you need to keep improving if you are to maintain—or, even better, <u>improve</u>—your position in your industry."

★ **Match the quality system to the application.** This was difficult, Marlow recalls. "I think the most difficult part for us was that the application questions searched for structured answers," he says. "Your quality system may be organized entirely differently so that what you have to do is to translate your system to answer their questions."

★ **Get the application done early.** "The applica-

tion was due the third of April, and we actually filed it a week ahead of time, even though we had to stay up all night to do it," Marlow says. "That was the schedule we had set up. The Wallace Company had cautioned us that it gets very hectic toward the end. We knew we needed to allow for that, so we did."

★ **Prepare thoroughly for the site visit.** Since Xerox, a member of the American Society for Quality Control (ASQC), is also in the Dallas area, people from Marlow Industries met with personnel from Xerox, Marlow reports. (See Xerox's own Baldrige quality success story, Chapter Three.) "They gave us an overview of what to expect, came back when we were about 90 percent through and talked again, and then came in one more time as we prepared for the site visit," he explains. "They asked us some 'dummy' questions just to let us know the types of questions the Baldrige Examiners might ask.

"We also had discussions with personnel from the Wallace Company," Marlow adds. "During a visit to Dallas, they told our employees what a site visit was like. Our Site Visit was on September 24 and 25." Of course, he notes, no one can give you the specific answers you'll need during a site visit, but they *can* give you an overview of what to expect.

MAKING IMPROVEMENTS LONG INTO THE FUTURE

On October 10, 1991, the Malcolm Baldrige National Quality Award winners for that year were announced. Three companies from the electronics industry won: Solectron Corporation and Zytec Corporation (both also profiled in this Chapter) in the manufacturing category and Marlow Industries in the small business category. The three were honored at a ceremony in Washington, D.C., on October 29.

"When we first set out [to establish a quality system], we planned on a long-term program," Marlow states. "We plan to continue to improve our Total Quality Management system, which is our top-to-bottom approach to customer satisfaction.

"Based on our feedback from our Baldrige application, we're estimating that we will have two years' worth of things we need to do in the area of continuous improvement. That's our plan."

"I think the important thing is that winning the Baldrige Award was not the challenge here," adds Witzke. "The voyage continues, and the Award was just a milestone along the way.

"Every year, the competition gets stiffer, and your customers' requirements increase. Therefore, every year, you need to keep improving if you are to maintain—or, even better, *improve*—your position in your industry," Witzke stresses.

Solectron Corporation

This fast-growing customized products manufacturer used the Baldrige application to fortify its already strong quality foundation—and then it actually became an Award recipient.

Solectron Corporation is a leading independent provider of customized integrated manufacturing services to original equipment manufacturers (OEMs) in the electronics industry. The company specializes in the assembly of complex printed circuit boards and subsystems for makers of computers and other electronic products. It also provides system-level assembly services of personal computers and mainframe mass storage subsystems, and it does turnkey materials management, board design, and manufacturability consultation and testing.

By most standards, Solectron is a young company; it was founded in 1977 as an assembly job shop with initial revenues of several hundred thousand dollars. By 1991, Solectron had become a $265-million-a-year business occupying approximately 750,000 square feet of building space in five locations in San Jose and Milpitas, California. (As of this writing, the company has plans to consolidate its locations onto a campus in the Milpitas area; in 1991, Solectron opened its first off-shore plant in Panang, Malaysia.)

How did this relatively new company achieve such rapid growth *and* join the ranks of Baldrige Award recipients? Part of Solectron's success lies in the fact that it used the Baldrige criteria to polish every facet of its already quality-conscious operation. Director of Quality Richard Allen shares with you some of the philosophies and actions that have caused the organization to achieve its enviable level of excellence.

CULTURE BASED ON CONTINUOUS IMPROVEMENT AND CUSTOMER SATISFACTION

"The Chief Executive Officer of Solectron, Dr. Winston Chen, has always been dedicated to quality, continuous improvement, and customer satisfaction," Allen reports. "So Dr. Chen has been the driving force of this philosophy in our organization. His focus has always been on customer satisfaction and reviving American competitiveness in manufacturing.

"As our company grew, Dr. Chen helped drive these philosophies down to every employee in the company," Allen continues. "From the very early days of the company's existence, he worked on the floor with the production people, and continued upward from there. He put together a lot of the initial training programs and was instrumental in implementing statistical process control throughout the whole company."

Allen notes that although larger companies often give sophisticated titles to their quality processes, Solectron has always kept it simple: "We simply call it our 'Quality Process' or 'Continuous Improvement Process' when we talk to our employees."

FLUCTUATING DEFECT RATES LED TO BALDRIGE CRITERIA

Although Solectron's level of defects was not high, it still wanted to see them decrease—preferably to the point where they were eliminated altogether. "As time went by, our defect rates dropped, but then they would level off," recalls Allen. "We had to figure out a method that would keep them continuously dropping. In addition, we were looking for a good improvement system that would affect *all* aspects of the company.

"We looked at Deming, Juran, and Crosby. Then we looked at the Baldrige criteria. It seemed as if the actual process of going through the Baldrige application and using the questions as a basis for improvement was a very good process. So we incorporated the whole process into our improvement strategy.

It should be stressed that Solectron's goal in applying the Baldrige criteria to its operation wasn't to win the Award, but to achieve continuous improvement throughout the organization. "We felt initially that the Award would be nice to win, but it was secondary to improving Solectron's quality. We had no plans to win when we first started to apply," Allen asserts. "We looked at the application completion and feedback as *an evolutionary process of improvement.* If we won the Award, it would be icing on the cake."

Award Winning Quality

Initially, Solectron brought in consultants to provide a basic understanding of what to do to meet the Baldrige criteria. "Three years ago, when we wrote our first application, we initially brought in three consultants to help us understand the application process. Dr. Thomas Kennedy, vice president of Quality and Engineering Technology, and I worked with the consultants for approximately two weeks to learn the Baldrige application process and what we had to do to apply. They explained how to answer the questions and the format that past applicants had used.

"During this time, the consultants also toured our facilities and reviewed many of our processes," Allen continues. "Before they left, they told us we had a pretty good story."

"Then we wrote our first application. The first year,

Tom and I were the primary writers of the application. We utilized an outside professional technical writer to help with technical writing and act as a wordsmith. We also used internal secretarial help for proofreading. As I generated the charts, Tom took on the role of editor for the entire application."

Allen explains that the Baldrige criteria examined seven critical areas: Leadership; Information and Analysis; Strategic Quality Planning; Human Resource Utilization; Quality Assurance of Products and Services; Quality Results; and Customer Satisfaction (there have been some changes in the criteria; see Chapter One). Applicants must answer specific questions within each category. Strong emphasis is placed on quality achievement and improvements based on quantitative data furnished by the applicants.

Many companies have sought the Baldrige Award, but few have won one because they cannot meet the stringent requirements of this self-examination. However, Solectron's philosophy had been quality and customer oriented from the start, and it had collected data in these areas through the years.

Each year, there were some changes in the application, notes Allen. "The application itself was noticeably different in the early stages from what it is now. It was more 'quality cited by example' in the first couple of years. Now, they are looking for you to show them your process and to show how you are working the process. So there's a big difference in the question structure." However, Allen says, these changes were to Solectron's advantage. "Because Solectron has always collected a lot of data, it wasn't too hard to go back to the early stages of the application process. We had a lot of the information. All we had to do was write about what we already had."

THE CUSTOMER DRIVES SOLECTRON'S QUALITY EFFORTS

Focusing on the customer is one factor that has helped Solectron gain its quality edge. "Everything is driven from the customer backward," Allen stresses. "As a contract manufacturing company, Solectron manufactures products designed by its customers. We compete on the basis of service, quality, and cost. Therefore, we go to great lengths to determine how existing and prospective customers define superior performance." How does Solectron gauge its customers' level of satisfaction with its products—and then assure their ongoing satisfaction? Here are some of the techniques it uses:

★ **Carry out weekly customer satisfaction polls.** "We have a very unique approach to understanding whether we are satisfying our customers," says Allen. "This approach has been ongoing since the early years of the company's existence. What we do every week is

to poll *every single* customer. We ask them to rate us in four different categories":

➤ **Quality**—How good was the quality of the product that we sent you?
➤ **Delivery**—Was our delivery on time? Did the product arrive in good shape?
➤ **Communication**—Are we returning your phone calls? Are we paying attention to your needs?
➤ **Service**—How good are we at meeting your needs? Are you happy with our service?

"Our customers are asked to provide a letter grade: A, B, C, or D for each of these categories each week. The first two categories, quality and delivery, are objective. The second two categories, communication and service, are subjective. We might be meeting their quality needs and we might be delivering their goods on time, but we are also concerned about how our customers *feel* about us and our products," Allen asserts.

"We use a very strict grading curve," he continues. "It works this way: Nothing is acceptable except an A. It gets negative from there. An A-minus is 90, B is 80, C is 0, and a D is minus 100. We pay a huge penalty for any customer that rates us at C (average) or lower in any category, because we do a straight average of all those numbers. So every week, we get all this information back and we average it out by customer.

"We also ask them for any comments they have on things we've done that they liked or didn't like. We record those comments *verbatim*. We have found that customers who don't 'feel' like they are getting good service often react to that emotionally, and we get the brunt of [their displeasure], so we believe it is important to react to their feelings.

"This information is gathered from the customers on Monday. On Tuesday, it all gets compiled, and that information goes back to the respective divisions that service those customers. They have to come up with answers to any negative comments or questions or grades. We essentially have to come up with an action plan every week as to what we did or didn't do for that customer the previous week.

"On Thursday morning at 7:30, we have a senior management staff meeting, which includes the CEO, the COO, all the vice presidents, directors, division managers, and a number of the managers and supervisors. In this large forum, we review the entire package every week. That way, the whole company gets to see what is going on with every single customer."

★ **Give customers feedback every week.** "We used to give our customers feedback by phone," Allen recalls. "Sometimes, we would send back a formal response in the form of an incident report.

"This year, however, we have formalized the process even more. Now we send back an actual customer complaint and resolution plan that lists the problem and what we're doing about it, gives the customer the time frame in which the problem will be corrected, and explains how it will be corrected. This package is then kept on record for future reference."

★ **Provide customer support.** At Solectron, customers are supported by two teams:

➤ *Customer Focus Teams.* "The purpose of these teams is to evaluate production for each customer," explains Allen. "Their goals are to prevent potential problems and to identify ways to improve process yields. "These teams meet with their customers weekly—at a minimum—and in a lot of cases, they meet more frequently than that.

"They put together and send a formal weekly report to the customers, which provides a snapshot status of what happened during the week with respect to schedules, quality, test yields, product deliveries, and any other open action items that need to be discussed. The teams and their customers mutually review and use the reports and any feedback to make sure that customers are continuously satisfied with the products being delivered. That report can be up to a half inch thick, to give you an idea of the amount of paperwork involved," Allen adds.

➤ *Project-Planning Teams.* "These teams work with customers in planning, scheduling, and defining material requirements," says Allen. "These teams' key concern is ensuring customer on-time delivery.

"The project-planning teams are really geared toward our turnkey-type customers, for whom we will actually buy all the parts, assemble them, and give them a finished product because there is a lot more to do for these customers," Allen continues.

"If there are special requirements for a customer, this team gets the right people together up-front so that the job can proceed quickly. As a normal course of events, when products are running, we have a customer focus team, which has people from Quality, Manufacturing, Engineering, and Scheduling—these key people are the ones who can assure that the product will continue to get to the customer on time, on an ongoing basis."

★ **Set up customized centers for specific customers.** "The assembly operations at Solectron are designed for specific customers' products, so the same people work on the same products over time," says Allen. "We don't have many high volume, standardized products. We have just the opposite; very short runs and a very high mix of products.

"If a customer has a large amount of work, we will create a division, essentially a P&L (profit and loss) center, for the customer. Otherwise, we'll create P&L

centers for a group of customers. We tend to staff divisions to be no larger than 200 or 300 people."

INSTITUTE A FORMAL QUALITY TRAINING PROGRAM

Many companies train their employees on a need-to-know basis. In other words, they teach them what they need to know to complete a certain job that comes in, but they don't have a comprehensive, quality-oriented training plan to ensure broader skills, knowledge, and comprehension. However, a formalized training plan is necessary to assure total quality and to meet the stringent Baldrige criteria.

"We used to have a training program based on needs," Allen says. "For instance, when someone needed to be trained on an assembly process, we'd work on developing the needed skills. We did not have a formal training program, which was something we were criticized for on our first application.

"To formalize our training program and give it direction, we created a position called vice president of training. This job was to assess the total training needs of the company from the lowest to the highest level and put in place a training program that would meet not only our current needs but our future needs as well." Here's a look at each element of Solectron's formalized training plan:

✧ **Quality-awareness training.** "We trained heavily in quality awareness," says Allen. "In these sessions, we included the Baldrige application and criteria training. We tried to make Baldrige-awareness training a part of everyone's daily job."

✧ **Management-leadership training.** "All senior management was next put through a management leadership training program. To do this, several of our instructors attended a 'train the trainer' program and taught the management leadership course to all our executives," Allen explains. "We are now teaching a more basic form of this course to our supervisors."

✧ **Technical training.** "It was also determined that we needed technical training in certain areas. At Solectron, we are fortunate to have a number of good technical experts. We have nine Ph.D.s in different disciplines, and these people helped develop courses to support our technical needs such as reliability, waste-solder processes, and board cleanliness. Seminar training is conducted for our technical staff to elevate its knowledge of our business."

✧ **Statistical process control (SPC) training.** "We offered SPC training at three levels: first, the operator level; second, the supervisory and engineering level, and third, advanced SPC techniques and design of experiments. This third level was strictly for the engineering groups. Practically everyone in the company, including the secretaries and administrative people, received the first-level statistical process control training," explains Allen.

To help eliminate defects—and also to encourage individual responsibility for quality—Solectron asks all its operators to do statistical analyses of their own work, generate control charts for their internal processes, and then correct any problems they uncover.

"Our operators are working in an area where there are a lot of small parts being assembled," Allen points out. "The statistical process controls that we put into place go right down to the operator level. They actually do self-corrections to the processes when they fluctuate beyond what is normal."

> "We trained heavily in quality awareness. In these sessions, we included the Baldrige application and criteria training. We tried to make Baldrige-awareness training a part of everyone's daily job."

All departments at Solectron are now required to use SPC regularly. SPC charts track performance of each machine with measurements recorded in an SPC database. Division quality managers and the corporate quality director track and review results daily. Since 1987, average product quality has improved. Here are two examples of SPC at work in two critical areas:

① **Solder monitoring:** "One of the very critical areas that we have to continually monitor is the actual solder applied to the circuit boards," Allen explains. "This is because the devices currently being used on circuit boards have very small leads and are soldered directly to the surface of the circuit board—they don't go through holes any more.

"The solder used is in the form of a solder paste. It's very critical how much of this paste is put on every pad. So every hour, the operators will actually take physical-height readings of that solder paste and then record those readings on control charts.

"If the height goes above a certain limit, we know the machine has gone out of control, the paste is

wrong, or something else is going amiss. By looking at the control charts, the operators can see early warning signs of possible problems. Corrections are then made to bring the process back under control."

② **Board cleanliness:** "Another critical area is the *cleanliness* of the boards," Allen reports. "We have found that the most critical components in our process are the raw PC boards—or printed circuit boards—without any components on them. If they are not clean, they will not hold solder, and the components won't become—or remain—soldered to the boards.

"Because of the complexity of the devices today, the spacing between components is very small, which makes it almost impossible to visually inspect for defects in the solder. All material has to be able to accept solder before we actually begin the solder process, so all bare-board lots are sampled for cleanliness and solderability," Allen explains. "As the solder process begins, we measure and monitor conveyor speed, temperature, and 10 to 15 other checkpoints in that process alone. These measurements are then recorded on statistical process control charts by operators.

"The operators are empowered to stop the line if they see any problems. If it is something that they don't understand, then they'll get an engineer or somebody else involved. In most cases, it is a minor adjustment that they can correct themselves."

CREATE AN ENVIRONMENT THAT ENCOURAGES A QUALITY ATTITUDE

Solectron takes several steps to create an environment in which all employees are encouraged to put quality first every day. Here's how it accomplishes this:

◆ **Give workers responsibility for meeting quality goals.** Solectron requires the support of its employees to meet its quality goals, notes Allen. So division managers go to their people and ask, "How are you going to meet these goals, and how will you do it as an operating division?"

"Many teams are created to help this process," Allen says. "Examples may include a production control team, a materials team, an operations team for soldering, or a team for auto-inserting parts. They all pull together to decide what we need to do."

◆ **Encourage a strong "family" atmosphere.** Solectron started out with a primarily Asian work force, but now has 2,200 employees representing over 20 different cultures, reports Allen. "Solectron's high-energy, customer-focused work force has developed a strong family orientation," he points out. "That initial corporate culture was set up when the company started, and it has grown and led each employee to have a positive attitude toward the person working next to him or her. We've had virtually no problems interculturally throughout the whole company."

◆ **Promote clear and effective communications.** Because of the many languages and dialects spoken at Solectron, the company finds communicating with its employees to be one of its key challenges. The company had to ensure a way to communicate effectively with its diverse work force.

"Almost everyone in the company speaks *some* English," says Allen. "To help everyone improve their English, the company offers ESL (English as a Second Language) courses on site through a local community college. To get information to our employees, training materials and other printed materials such as publications or announcements are published in four languages: English, Spanish, Chinese, and Vietnamese."

◆ **Implement a recognition and reward program.** "In most cases, we give rewards and recognition to groups, rather than individuals," says Allen. "We have only two or three individualized awards, given for exceptional performance for a specific task.

"On a quarterly basis, we may give out two or three awards to specific groups. This is usually done by our CEO, Dr. Winston Chen, or our president, Dr. Ko Nishim. Recognition may be given because a customer has called up to praise the customer focus team that has been working with it and that has done an exceptional job. These types of actions trigger our executive management to publicly reward that group of people.

Other ways management rewards groups include:

⇨ **Buying a whole division lunch**
⇨ **Bringing in ice cream for the entire corporation or the entire operation**
⇨ **Providing monetary rewards to a complete operating division**
⇨ **Giving monetary rewards to an improvement team**

THE QUALITY JOURNEY KNOWS NO END

Although Solectron has joined the winner's circle of Baldrige winners, it is hardly resting on its laurels. The company aims to improve its products and processes *continuously*, aiming toward ever-tougher quality goals. "We've defined our goals through 1995. These include goals for on-time delivery, customer satisfaction, number of hours of training, how we want to look at our suppliers, and how we want to measure them," says Allen. "This way, we know what must be achieved at all times.

"After our goals are set, we meet with the division general managers and the quality managers to determine how best to meet these goals and what support from upper-level management is required. A plan is then put together that defines what is needed in terms of equipment, work force, training, and so forth. Then we work together to meet those goals.

"One of our goals is to achieve Six Sigma quality in all critical processes," Allen continues. (For an explanation of Six Sigma, see section on Motorola, Chapter Two, Figure 2-1.) "In some cases, we're at Three Sigma, and other cases we are up to Five Sigma. We're currently on track to where we think we should be, and we are continuing to use the Malcolm Baldrige guidelines and our other continuous-improvement methods to reach our Six Sigma target.

"Some of the challenges we are facing include the fact that the boards are getting more complex and customer requirements are getting tougher," Allen continues. "To remain a leader in quality, we need to further reduce our rejects and internal errors to less than 10 parts per million (ppm). We don't believe we are anywhere near where we need to be.

"We'll continue to follow the Baldrige criteria because we feel that they are an excellent road map to world-class quality and customer satisfaction. They can be applied to all areas of the company—not only in manufacturing, but in areas such as finance, human resources, and material procurement as well. Our goal is to have *every single area and every single process* at the Six Sigma level, with zero defects."

Solectron has won over 37 awards for superior customer satisfaction over the last 10 years, many of these since 1990. After a recent quality audit, a major customer rated Solectron as the "Best contract manufacturer of electronic assemblies in the United States."

"We've seen tremendous results in customer satisfaction and quality over the past three years by following the Malcolm Baldrige Award guidelines," Allen reports. "Defect rates have dropped substantially, and currently fall within the Five Sigma range, or 233 parts per million. On-time delivery to customers is at 97.7 percent."

He notes that 90 percent of new business comes from established customers, and many have closed their internal assembly operations after determining that Solectron can assemble better quality products at a lower price than they can. "The goal we're driving for is to be a billion-dollar corporation at the world-class level within three years," Allen points out.

But it isn't just *external* customers and their business that Solectron is concerned about. The company is committed to quality for its *internal* customers—its employees—too. "We are very dedicated to quality and making things better for everyone—our customers *and employees* alike," Allen stresses. "Solectron is very much aware that the whole winning of the Award was accomplished through the combination of the work and efforts of *everyone* at the company."

Zytec Corporation

A methodical "Management By Planning" strategy—combined with the Baldrige criteria—helped this successful company to establish continuous quality goals and keep them consistent throughout its organization.

Zytec Corporation (Eden Prairie, MN) has its manufacturing facility in Redwood Falls, MN, 96 miles from its Eden Prairie headquarters. At the facility, 654 of Zytec's 748 workers manufacture power supplies for original equipment manufacturers of computers and for electronic office, medical, and testing equipment. (This accounts for 90 percent of its revenues, which totaled $50 million in 1990. The other 10 percent, totaling $5.8 million in 1990, comes from its repair of cathode-ray tube monitors and power supplies. The power-supply repair service is the largest of its kind in the United States.)

Originally a unit of Magnetic Peripherals Inc., Zytec began operating independently in 1984, following a leveraged buyout. In seven years, the company rose to the top tier of the hundreds of manufacturers of power supplies for electronic equipment in the United States. And to top it all off, Zytec was given the prestigious Baldrige Award in 1991.

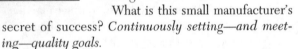

What is this small manufacturer's secret of success? *Continuously setting—and meeting—quality goals.*

"We have been on a quality journey since shortly after we started Zytec in 1984," explains Ronald D. Schmidt, Chairman, President and CEO. "We don't have a quality *program*, we have a quality *culture*. [As part of that culture] we have been driving Deming's 14 points for management since the summer of 1984." (See box at the end of this section.)

In 1988, however, Schmidt and his senior staff began to feel that their efforts toward continuous quality improvement were reaching a plateau. So they began to search for other processes through which they could continually stimulate and motivate their entire work force.

Here's how Zytec attained its continuous quality objectives.

PUTTING MANAGEMENT BY PLANNING AND BALDRIGE APPLICATION TO WORK

The first process Schmidt and his senior staff looked at was called Management By Planning. "Management By Planning is a process that's probably different from those used at most other companies," Schmidt says. "It's a takeoff on Hoshan Kanri—which is a Japanese process-oriented MBO [management by objectives] system. Our vice president of Marketing and Sales and I went to Japan in 1988 on a TQC [Total Quality Control] study mission to learn more about Hoshan Kanri.

"With Deming, you don't set arbitrary numbers or goals, so I was struggling with how to do that. I was trying to come up with a way in which we could set goals that people wanted and needed, but which I didn't arbitrarily set. I was hoping this visit would help us to do that.

"Upon returning from Japan, our Chief Financial Officer and I attended a training class put on by GOAL/QPC on Management By Planning. He and I later taught the Management By Planning process to everyone on our management team. We adopted this method because it involved employees in setting both long-term and yearly goals."

Also in 1988, Schmidt says, "I started looking for something to motivate us still further. At that time, I evaluated the Baldrige application to see if it would provide us with another incentive to work on. I also was interested in seeing whether it was consistent enough with Deming's philosophies so that it would not confuse our people."

Although Schmidt was interested in the Baldrige application in 1988, his senior staff was not interested in doing anything with it until 1989. At that time, he says, "My senior staff agreed that the Baldrige application was worthwhile and consistent with our culture. We decided that we would use it as another way of measuring ourselves."

> **"My senior staff agreed that the Baldrige application was worthwhile and consistent with our culture. We decided that we would use it as another way of measuring ourselves."**

This led Schmidt and his staff to commit themselves—in the presence of their employees—to the fact that Zytec was going for the Baldrige, and that it was going to win the Award in the next five years.

CONTINUOUS IMPROVEMENT THROUGH MANAGEMENT BY PLANNING

As staffers became familiar with the Baldrige application and incorporated the criteria into their operations, Zytec used the interactive Management By Planning process to ensure that the entire work force was consistently focusing on the same quality goals. Here's a look at this step-by-step process:

✪ **Step 1: The executive staff defines strategic issues.** "The executive staff started our long-range planning cycle by defining the strategic issues we would have to address in the next five years to be a prosperous company," says Schmidt.

✪ **Step 2: Cross-functional teams prepare five-year plans.** "Then we assigned six cross-functional teams to prepare five-year plans based on the strategic issues we give them. These six teams represent functional areas of the company including Marketing, Technology, Manufacturing, Materials, the Product Renewal Center, and the corporation.

"We had 54 cross-functional employees involved in those six teams in 1991. These teams address the strategic issues derived by the senior staff, and they may suggest other strategic issues based on needs of their particular areas," Schmidt notes.

✪ **Step 3: Senior staff critiques proposed goals.** "The six teams then come back and report their respective five-year visions to the senior staff. The senior staff reviews the goals simply to see whether all six teams are headed in the same direction. We don't fine-tune anything at that point in time," says Schmidt.

✪ **Step 4: Employees, customers, and suppliers critique goals.** "If the goals look all right, we set up two meetings off site where we invite employee representatives from each area, as well as customers and supplier representatives. The six teams present their findings to the people at this meeting. What we're looking for are inconsistencies, such as Quality going in one way and Manufacturing going in another.

"After the six teams present their reports, we ask the people attending the meetings to go off in their own groups and come up with a consensus critique of what they have just heard. Then they make a presentation of their findings."

✪ **Step 5: Senior staff generates long- and short-term strategic plans.** "Following these meetings, the senior staff generates a long-range strategic plan document that covers the next five years. They also set broad corporate objectives to guide quality planning in the departments," Schmidt explains.

"In addition, the senior staff decides which items are still strategic action items that need to be acted upon in the immediate future. They then review those on a quarterly basis to try to bring them to a conclusion. They also come up with four key corporate short-term, one-year objectives."

✪ **Step 6: Areas in company set one-year goals.** The four key corporate short-term, one-year objectives are then sent to the individual areas in the company, which are asked to set up their own one-year goals based on what they can do to support the company's objectives in those four areas.

"First, the teams set up their own objectives," says Schmidt. "Then, I meet with each team personally and help them establish their objectives. I do a little coaching if I feel they are being too aggressive or not aggressive enough; but basically, we tie in to what their objectives are.

"They define how they are going to measure and track their objectives. They define an action plan they'll use to meet them. Then, they report their progress at our monthly operations review. We get objectives set throughout the company, and we have them tied back to our five-year plan. We have everyone going in the same direction."

KEEPING EMPLOYEES MOTIVATED HELPS KEEP QUALITY ON TRACK

How does Zytec involve and motivate its employees to help keep the quality plans on track? Here are some of the techniques it uses:

✷ **Assign interdepartmental teams to design and develop new products.** Cross-functional teams work closely with customers at four key stages in the design and development of new products: predesign initiation, design initiation, prototype delivery and testing, and preproduction certification. The teams are empowered to make all decisions, including setting critical parameters for measurement and control.

In addition to the design teams, there are self-managed teams: Several departments at Zytec are now overseen by self-directed teams.

✷ **Empower employees through training.** All employees receive quality-related training in analytical and problem-solving methods. Various levels of training are offered as employees continue to advance in their skill levels.

✷ **Develop skills with a Multifunctional Employee Program.** To encourage employees to further improve their job skills and to gain more flexibility after basic training, Zytec has initiated the Multifunctional Employee program (MFE), through which employees are rewarded for the number of job skills they acquire.

✶ **Institute employee recognition/suggestion program.** "We have an employee recognition/suggestion program, which we call the Implemented Improvement System (IIS)," says Schmidt. "It's a takeoff on a Japanese concept."

The IIS works in this manner: "When employees come up with an idea that they want to change something, they need to get only one person's approval, and that's from their supervisor. Once they've secured that, they are totally responsible for implementing whatever their idea is. They are free to talk to our suppliers or go to the maintenance or engineering departments or other areas to get something done. They don't get credit for their idea unless it's implemented."

> **"We get objectives set throughout the company, and we have them tied back to our five-year plan. We have everyone going in the same direction."**

"When an employee's idea is implemented, he or she gets one dollar. Then, we have a group of peers select the best improvement ideas that were implemented each month, and the first-place winners receive $100, second place $75, and third place $50. We've recently implemented the same process in the safety area."

Although employees appreciate the cash rewards, their *favorite* acknowledgment is not financial, according to Schmidt. "The reward the employees seem to like best is rather unique with our company. It works like this: When our employees turn in suggestions, their names go into a hat. The peer-review team draws out a name each month and that person gets a day off with pay."

But here's the unique part: "The employees whose names are chosen have the right to ask anyone in the company to do their work for them on that day," Schmidt explains. "They often take their days off with pay, but then come in to watch the person who has to do their job.

"Sometimes, that person is me," Schmidt admits.

PERFORMANCE MEASUREMENT AND SUPPLIER PARTNERSHIPS

Another aspect of Zytec's quality process is forging beneficial relationships with other companies. It does this through supplier partnerships and benchmarking:

✦ **Supplier partnerships.** "One of our objectives is to form partnerships with our suppliers," says Schmidt. "However, we're not experts at this yet."

To help form these partnerships, Zytec holds "supplier days," where suppliers and Zytec people get together to discuss goals, problems, and solutions. "In fact, I announced our Baldrige win at our supplier day. We had a large room full of suppliers and employees when I announced it, and it was an exciting time for everybody."

✦ **Benchmarking.** Because it is data driven, Zytec has developed meaningful, measurable internal criteria for evaluating performance at all levels of the company. It also measures its performance by benchmarking leading industries that have achieved world-class, "best practice" status in key manufacturing and human resource areas. Zytec studies these other companies' operations, and in so doing, learns how it can improve its own processes.

GOING FOR THE BALDRIGE: ONCE YOU START, THERE'S NO TURNING BACK

The first time Zytec applied for the Baldrige Award was in 1990, Schmidt reports. "In 1990, we split up the seven sections of the application among the staff members," says Schmidt. "Each section was assigned to several people. Each person was to document what they did in each area and write it up. When we had all seven sections done, we were going to look at the finished application to see whether we thought it was worth submitting.

"Once we got into the process, we decided there was no turning back and that we would go for it. We thought that even if we didn't win, we would get value for our efforts because the examiner's feedback would help us evaluate our strengths and weaknesses.

"The data used for the application were already available in the company, so all we did was document what we were currently doing," Schmidt continues. "However, we sometimes found that we had no good answers to the questions on the application, which was shocking to us. In areas where we didn't have good answers, we made some changes."

One problem Schmidt and his staffers had in processing the paperwork was a lack of time. It takes a great deal of time, thought, research, and effort to properly process a Baldrige application. "One of our key problems was getting time to document and write our parts of the application because everyone had to do it on top of their regular job responsibilities. This was not an easy process. To get the application done, we ended up working around the clock and on weekends. We used no consultants for this process."

> "[Winning the Baldrige] is kind of a wayside rest in our journey. We're going to stop and smell the roses a little bit, but then we're going right back out on the road, because we know we have a lot of improvement to do yet."

As each person completed his or her documentation and write-up, Schmidt acted as the editor. He says, "I broke it down to the right size and made it look like it came from the same company. We completed the 1990 Baldrige application by around 5:30 a.m. on the day it was due.

"We were one of 15 manufacturing companies to make it through a Stage One Review," Schmidt reports. "In a Stage One Review, the examiners review key areas, not the whole report. This examination determines if it is worthwhile for them to do a full review.

"When they cut it down to the six companies that got a site visit in 1990, we lost out," says Schmidt. "We felt pretty good, though. We thought, 'Well, we'll take the data we got from this review. We'll make some changes, and we'll shoot for a site visit in 1991.'"

CRITICAL CHANGES LEAD TO SUCCESS THE SECOND TIME AROUND

Zytec changed its approach somewhat for the 1991 application. First of all, one person was made responsible for the completion of each section. "In 1990, we had more than one person responsible for a section," Schmidt notes. "In 1991, however, we decided that someone has to be responsible for each of the seven sections. They could get help if they wanted it, but they were held responsible for getting it done. Several

of the staff went down deeper into the organization and had some of their people write the technical information needed."

In addition, a writer was hired to put the sections together in a uniform fashion. "This time, I was editor again—but I did hire a writer; I'm an engineer, not a writer," Schmidt says. "This proved to be difficult, however, because the writer would use the right verbiage, but didn't always say exactly what we wanted to have said. We ended up reworking each other's work a lot. However, I think we ended up with a better document because of it.

"We also tried to portion out the pages by saying, 'You got 30 percent of the points, so you have 30 percent of the pages.' Still we had a hard time boiling the information down to fit in 75 pages," Schmidt admits.

The second time around, Zytec got its application done with time to spare. "Again, we found this was not an easy process; especially when you have to do it on top of your regular work load. But still it can be done. You don't have to hire consultants or have people working full-time on it."

This time Zytec got through the Stage Two Review and was notified that it was going to get a site visit. So people would be ready for the site visit, each section of the application was reduced in size and published in the weekly editions of the employee newsletter.

THE REWARDS FOR SUPERIOR QUALITY KEEP ON ROLLING IN

"In 1991, the state of Minnesota came up with a quality award patterned after the Baldrige," Schmidt reports. "The application for this was due a week after the Baldrige application. We took the Baldrige and cut it down. Instead of the 75 pages maximum allowed by the Baldrige committee, we had to trim our information still further, so it fit onto 35 pages. The Director of Quality and my secretary edited it and submitted it to Minnesota."

"The Minnesota site visit happened prior to the Baldrige," Schmidt continues. "All we did to prepare our people for this was to spend about an hour with everyone prior to the visit. We wanted our people to be themselves and to be honest. We explained that visitors were coming in. We told them that the visitors would want them to be factual, and that they were friends, not enemies. We told them to tell the truth and be themselves. So we didn't spend a lot of time with our people before the site visit." And apparently, they didn't need to—Zytec received the Minnesota Quality Award in addition to the Baldrige.

"As I mentioned, Minnesota's award was patterned after the Baldrige, with the same potential six winners. We were the only company that was awarded the Minnesota Quality Award. That was a bit overwhelming," Schmidt concedes.

Zytec has enjoyed many business successes beyond winning a couple of very prestigious quality awards. For example, the company's new business has achieved double-digit annual growth in the last three years. Sales per employee are approaching $100,000—as compared with an industry average of less than $80,000.

Since 1988, Zytec has also enjoyed the following benefits of its quality process:

➤ **50 percent improvement in manufacturing yields**

➤ **26 percent reduction in manufacturing cycle time**

➤ **50 percent reduction in the design cycle**

➤ **30 to 40 percent decrease in product costs**

Of course, winning the Baldrige Award probably ranks up there as the peak experience for everyone at the company. "I'm really happy for our employees," says Schmidt. "We've worked hard and we've got super people." Although people at Zytec are naturally elated about winning the Award, however, they know that they've hardly reached the end of the road to quality.

"[Winning the Baldrige] is kind of a wayside rest in our journey," Schmidt points out. "We're going to stop and smell the roses a little bit, but then we're going right back out on the road, because we know we have a lot of improvement to do yet."

Deming's 14 Points of Management Obligations

Dr. W. Edwards Deming's quality teachings in Japan from 1950 on helped the Japanese transform their business strategies, projecting them into worldwide prominence as the leader in producing quality products. His program was primarily statistical in its orientation, but he also developed some cogent management concepts, which are embodied in his "14 Points of Management Obligations."

Here is an overview of the 14 points, which apply to both small and large organizations, to divisions within companies, and to service as well as manufacturing organizations:

★ 1. Create constancy of purpose toward improvement of product and service, with the aim to become competitive and stay in business, and to provide jobs.

★ 2. Adopt this new philosophy: We are in a new economic age created by Japan. Transformation of Western management style is necessary to halt the continued decline of industry.

★ 3. Cease depending on inspection to achieve quality. Eliminate the need for inspection on a mass basis by building quality into the product in the first place.

★ 4. End the practice of awarding business on the basis of price tag. Purchasing must be combined with design of product, manufacturing, and sales to work with the chosen suppliers; the aim is to minimize total cost, not merely initial cost.

★ 5. Improve constantly and forever every activity in the company in order to improve quality and productivity and thus constantly decrease costs.

★ 6. Institute training and education on the job for everyone, including management.

★ 7. Institute supervision. The aim of supervision should be to help people and machines do a better job.

★ 8. Drive out fear so that everyone may work effectively for the company.

★ 9. Break down barriers between departments. People in Research, Design, Sales, and Production must work as a team to tackle usage and production problems that may be encountered with the product or service.

★ 10. Eliminate slogans, exhortations, and targets for the work force that ask for zero defects and new levels of productivity. Such exhortations only create adversarial relationships; the bulk of the causes of low quality and low productivity belongs to the system and thus lies beyond the power of the work force.

★ 11. Eliminate work standards that prescribe numerical quotas for the day. Substitute aids and helpful supervision.

★ 12a. Remove the barriers that rob hourly workers of the right to pride of workmanship. The responsibility of supervisors must be changed from sheer numbers to quality.

★ 12b. Remove the barriers that rob people in management and in engineering of their right to pride of workmanship. This means, among other things, abolition of the annual or merit rating and of management by objective.

★ 13. Institute a vigorous program of education and retraining. New skills are required for changes in techniques, materials, and service.

★ 14. Put everybody in the company to work in teams to accomplish the transformation.

Chapter Six

**Quality Improvement the Baldrige Way:
Even Without the Trophy, Your Company Can Become a Winner!**

Being selected to receive a Malcolm Baldrige National Quality Award is indeed a thrilling, rewarding experience for the companies that work hard to meet the tough criteria, go through the rigorous application process, and join the winner's circle each year. However, scores of firms are learning that you don't have to have a Baldrige Award in your trophy cabinet to benefit from the Baldrige process. In fact, you don't even necessarily have to apply for the Award to begin learning valuable lessons about quality—you can start on the road to improvement just by studying the criteria (see Chapter One) and then developing creative ways to incorporate them into your quality plan. In this Chapter, we'll take a look at several companies that are becoming quality winners through their Baldrige-based efforts.

AT&T

Using the Baldrige criteria as its foundation, this industry giant built its own internal quality award process, which recognizes both achievement and improvement (and encourages more of the same).

In 1983, with the divestiture of the Bell telephone companies, AT&T lost its monopoly on telephone services. This led the company to a vigorous new interest in determining how to remain competitive in the marketplace—with the goal of surpassing all others in customer satisfaction.

AT&T tackled this challenge by offering a number of exciting new products and services. Today, its telecommunications services account for 50 percent of its revenues. Through Network Systems, AT&T provides network telecommunications products worldwide. The five Network Systems business units include switching, transmissions, operations, and cellular systems. AT&T is also involved in many other markets, such as financial services; designing, manufacturing, selling, and leasing communications products and services for the home; and developing and marketing business communication systems. In addition, AT&T designs and manufactures military equipment to meet federal government needs.

The company's diverse business units are at the top of its organizational structure. They are supported by corporate organizations and operating divisions. A Management Executive Committee sets corporate policy and strategy, while an Operations Committee assures implementation and monitors results. Group executives support the business units and their organizations and divisions.

AT&T's yearly revenues are $37 billion. Its employees number 275,000, with the NCR purchase adding about another 55,000. In addition, the organization is international in scope. Assuring excellence throughout this enormous operation is clearly a monumental task. To help motivate all staffers toward quality improvement, AT&T has developed a Baldrige-based quality award program.

"In 1990, we established the AT&T Chairman's Quality Award (CQA) process, which is our own internal version of the Baldrige process," explains Dale H. Myers, manager of Quality Planning at AT&T's Corporate Quality Office (Berkeley Heights, NJ). "We modeled it almost verbatim on the Baldrige. We used the same criteria and a similar examination process."

The CQA criteria are also incorporating the ISO (International Standards Organization) 9000 criteria, as all units doing business with the European market will need this accreditation. So when a unit of AT&T wins the CQA, the same information can be used to apply for both the Baldrige Award and for ISO 9000 accreditation.

THE CQA IS VIEWED AS "ICING ON THE CAKE"

The Chairman's Quality Award came about in 1990, when AT&T's chairman set three priorities for the organization:

⇨ **First,** to step up their efforts to have the best quality in the world.

⇨ **Second,** to keep striving for an operating style and behavior that focused more sharply on customer needs.

⇨ **Third,** to continue to develop into a truly global corporation.

The Baldrige criteria were to be adopted and used to assess AT&T's progress toward being acknowledged "best in the world" by its customers.

"When the proposal to create the Chairman's Quality Award was made, it was very clear to top management that they weren't really after the award itself," explains Myers. "The real reason they wanted [to establish the award] was because they believed it would help them to improve the bottom line, become more successful, improve customer satisfaction, and lower their costs. If they get the award, that's icing on the cake."

Award Winning Quality

THE OBJECTIVES OF AT&T'S CHAIRMAN'S QUALITY AWARD

The CQA is set up to recognize AT&T's business units and divisions. The annual awards were established to accomplish the following seven goals:

➤ **To promote awareness of quality as a strategic competitive approach**

➤ **To establish criteria for quality excellence within AT&T**

➤ **To recognize business units and divisions that excel in quality**

➤ **To encourage sharing of successful business units' and divisions' strategies and benefits**

➤ **To provide constructive feedback to business units and divisions to aid them in implementing a total quality approach to winning in the market**

➤ **To accelerate AT&T's rate of improvement toward becoming a leader in quality**

➤ **To serve as the selection process for an AT&T submittal to the Malcolm Baldrige National Quality Award**

Any AT&T unit that wishes to apply for the Baldrige Award must first apply for the Chairman's Quality Award. "Each unit has to go through the Chairman's Award Process before it can apply for the Baldrige, so that we can get a chance to thoroughly analyze and evaluate how they are doing in their quality system," Myers explains.

AT&T collects the analyses of the units that apply for the CQA each year. This information is used as input to determine who will be AT&T's Baldrige candidates for the following year.

At the beginning of the next year, the units that wish to be considered for the Baldrige make themselves known. The company takes the previous year's CQA analyses and updates current information. "Then the AT&T Corporate Quality Vice President takes that information and makes recommendations to our chairman and senior management team," Myers notes.

REWARDING NOT JUST ACHIEVEMENT BUT IMPROVEMENT AS WELL

Although the CQA is based on the Baldrige criteria, it takes that award process even further; it rewards not just those units that attain stringent quality standards but those that show specific degrees of quality *improvement*. The idea is to motivate and encourage *all* units to participate in the evaluation and self-improvement process, even if they might only be at the beginner's level.

"The Baldrige Award is designed around achievement," Myers points out. "It is trying to pick out the very best role models for U.S. industry. However, if you have business units that are just getting started or that are early in their programs, you may have a problem motivating a unit to participate [in the Baldrige process] because they're afraid they will get a low score. So we added a new wrinkle.

"We do have the achievement awards, which have threshold levels with corresponding bronze, silver, and gold awards. But we also have bronze, silver, and gold *improvement* awards for improving a minimum 100, 150, or 200 points respectively over the previous year's score. "So for those in the early stages of their quality system improvement journey, there is an incentive to jump and get a baseline and then work toward improving their quality systems over the next year."

RECOGNIZING THREE LEVELS OF ACHIEVEMENT AND IMPROVEMENT

Here's a look at the three levels of quality achievement and improvement, and the corresponding point values that they must receive from the evaluating committee:

	Achievement	Improvement
★ **Gold**	876-1,000 points	200 points/year
★ **Silver**	751-875 points	150 points/year
★ **Bronze**	600-750 points	100 points/year

To win a CQA, an applicant must meet these four requirements:

❶ *Attain a point score for the Application Report that satisfies an award category*
❷ *Substantiate during a site visit the programs that were described in the Application Report*
❸ *Be recommended by the panel of judges and approved by the Management Executive Committee*
❹ *Act as a role model for the corporation*

"Another difference between the Baldrige and our Chairman's Award is that there is no limit to the number of CQAs given," notes Myers. "The Baldrige has limited the number of awards because it is really trying to pick out and recognize the best. However, we recognize *every* unit that meets the criteria for an achievement or improvement award.

"Ideally, we'd like to hand out an award for every single business unit and division in the company," he adds. "What we are trying to do is to motivate and encourage people to continuously improve."

CQA SCHEDULE CLOSELY FOLLOWS THE BALDRIGE SCHEDULE

The AT&T Chairman's Quality Award schedule closely follows that for the Baldrige. For example, here is an overview of the 1991 CQA schedule:

January	*Board of Examiners selected*
February to April	*Board of Examiners trained*
April 1	*Letter of intent to apply due*
June 3	*Application package due*
June to August	*Application Report examined*
July	*Notification of site visit*
August 5-16	*Suggested target dates for site visit*
August 16	*Site visit completed*
October 1	*Feedback Report distributed*
October 28-29	*Recognition/Awards Ceremony*
November/ December	*Award Ceremony*

Business units interested in applying for the CQA must first notify the Corporate Quality Office and obtain approval to apply from the Management Executive Committee. When their plans have been approved, they must submit a written Application Report satisfying the criteria. In responding to these criteria, applicants are to provide information and data to substantiate and demonstrate the results of their efforts.

Who gathers the information and writes the applications? "That varies just as it does with the Baldrige Award," Myers replies. "We have the equivalent of the situation involving Ken Leach at Globe Metallurgical, where a quality manager was on the job a long time, knew the business well, did the first draft himself, and then circulated it and got lots of feedback.

"Some of our larger units formed cross functional teams with representatives from each of the key functions and operations within the business unit. There again, we have a wide spectrum on how the applications were put together. In one case, we had a division manager who took a personal interest and so wrote most of it himself.

"Some of the application teams have become an ongoing normal part of the business," Myers notes. "It is their job to help the senior management teams of their units use the feedback to improve their units' quality systems. Not all the business units have institutionalized the process yet. It's more of a one-time project for some; they do it and then the team disperses. So we have some variations here."

THE CQA CRITERIA ARE IDENTICAL TO THE BALDRIGE CRITERIA

"The examination criteria of the Chairman's Quality Award are identical to the Baldrige criteria," explains Myers. "The Baldrige Award Guidelines are inserted into the Chairman's Application Package, as published by the National Institute for Standards & Technology. Then we have an additional booklet that is specific to our process and includes our supplemental criteria.

"We try to stay as close as possible to the Baldrige application process, but modify the process when needed to address AT&T issues," he adds.

HOW THE CQA EXAMINATION PROCESS WORKS AT AT&T

The CQA examiners are specially trained AT&T employees, Myers points out. "We've trained our own internal board of examiners. In 1991, we had about 180." The examiners are chosen for their broad-based business and quality expertise.

They must volunteer by applying to be examiners, and then they must be trained each year. Most of them perform their examiner duties on top of their regular job, on their own time. Usually, the only time they do get official time releases is for site visits during normal working hours.

Each examiner independently reviews the Application Reports, documenting strengths, areas for improvement, and giving a numerical score for the applications. The examination team then develops a consensus report on their findings.

If an applicant qualifies for a site visit, the examination team visits some of the applicant's sites to clarify and verify information contained in the Application Report. The senior examiner then prepares a feedback report identifying major strengths and areas for improvement, and providing a baseline point score.

Each examining team has an experienced leader, a senior examiner who is a recognized leader in business and quality. These leaders coordinate the scoring of the individual examiners, and develop a consensus score. They also plan site visits with the applicant's coordinator, and write the feedback report.

The amount of feedback the CQA examiners generate is greater than that provided by the Baldrige examiners, Myers notes. "One unique thing about our process is the communication between the examiners and the applicants. Not only do applicants get a *written* feedback report but if they request it, we also expect the senior examiner on the examination team to give a *verbal* presentation, explaining the feedback report results to the applicant's senior management team. It's all geared toward maximizing the improvement efforts of the business unit."

Myers explains that judges evaluate the examiners' feedback reports. These judges are senior executives from business units and divisions, and are either leaders in quality or members of the Baldrige Award Board of Examiners. The judges then recommend CQA winners for Management Executive Committee approval. A Board of Trustees oversees the entire process. This Board ensures that the CQA is meeting its objectives, and that the award is properly supported. Trustees include the chairman, business unit presidents and division heads from Manufacturing and Service as well as nationally recognized quality leaders, such as Joseph Juran, Bonnie Small, and a Malcolm Baldrige senior examiner. This Management Executive Committee approves all CQA recipients.

UTILIZING FEEDBACK: IDENTIFYING STRENGTHS AND WEAKNESSES

"AT&T is moving to a decentralized management structure, where each of the business units pretty much run their own businesses," Myers explains. "As an example of how we implement the feedback for business unit improvement following the annual CQA process, we need to get a companywide view:

"Suppose *all* the units apply for the CQA, and we get a lot of feedback from each business unit. What we then do on a companywide basis is to try to identify the common strengths and the common areas for improvement. That information is then provided to our AT&T senior management team. They review this information to determine what they need to do to support all the businesses.

"A month ago, we completed the CQA process, and the business units got their feedback. We are now starting to do the systemic analysis—looking for the common strengths and the common weaknesses. At the same time, the business units' senior management teams are taking their feedback from the Baldrige report and are starting to do the same thing at their level. We will issue an annual AT&T status report, in which we carry out the following tasks":

- ◆ *Document the major issues to be addressed*
- ◆ *Identify and address some initiatives relating to these issues*
- ◆ *Set some targets*
- ◆ *Review these targets with the senior management team*
- ◆ *Distribute this information to all the presidents and heads of the business divisions, and also to all the quality managers in each of the divisions*

"At the business unit level, each business unit has a quality manager that is responsible for implementing the quality system within that unit. It is the responsibility of the units' quality managers to facilitate the use of the feedback reports from the CQA process.

"They review that with the senior management team and go through the process of identifying and prioritizing what they need to do. Then they help develop a quality system improvement plan."

MEET THE 1991 CQA WINNERS

Myers reports that in 1991, there were four CQA winners at AT&T:

✪ **AT&T Universal Card Services** won the Gold Improvement Award by providing superior customer service. The group placed fourth in a consumer survey that ranked 130 brands by user satisfaction, and was rated at the top in seven out of eight industry attributes for the credit card business.

✪ **Information Management Services** won a Bronze Improvement Award by defining and deploying a set of values that balanced the needs of customers, stockholders, and employees. It then simultaneously reduced overall costs by 15 percent per year, while improving the quality of customer service.

✪ **Switching Systems** won a Bronze Improvement Award for improvements made between 1988 and 1990 on the 4ESS(R) switch and the 5ESS(R) switch, and improving customer report card ratings.

✪ **Transmission Systems** also won a Bronze Improvement Award by achieving a 50 percent reduction in product realization intervals for new systems and driving the product quality level of purchased integrated circuit components from 1,700 parts per million in 1980 to 22 parts per million in 1990.

CQA winners are recognized in a special ceremony, as the Baldrige winners are. "Just as the Baldrige has a special recognition ceremony in Washington, AT&T has an annual AT&T quality conference that takes place at the end of October," says Myers. "That is the one time at AT&T where we bring together the quality community, business leaders, and senior officers from across the whole company.

"The chairman presents the award plaques to the head of the business unit or the division head, and the quality manager. The two managers receive the award as a team. Again, we're trying to encourage that need for business leaders and the quality community to form partnerships and to work together."

"We also hold an awards dinner that members of the Management Executive Committee attend to meet personally with the winning teams' president or business head, and the quality manager. At that dinner, the winners have the opportunity to share their successful strategies with AT&T's senior management team.

"This helps the senior managers better understand how they can support the improvement efforts in other business units and divisions. It's a two-way exchange—the winners receive recognition and our officers receive additional insight on successful strategies that they can encourage throughout AT&T."

CQA FOLLOW-UP: THE QUALITY SYSTEM CONTINUOUS IMPROVEMENT CYCLE

In the continuous improvement process that follows the annual feedback received from the CQA, AT&T applies the principles of the Shewhart Cycle, or Plan-Do-Check-Act (PDCA) Cycle (strongly advocated by quality expert W. Edwards Deming). This cycle traditionally involves the following steps:

1. **Plan** a change or test aimed at improvement.
2. **Do** the test, or try out the change, preferably on a small scale.
3. **Check** the results. Was the test or change successful?
4. **Act**: If the change or test *was* successful, adopt it and make it a part of the operation. If it was unsuccessful, abandon it, or run it again under different conditions to try to work out the variables that are getting in the way of a positive outcome.

Myers explains this cycle as applied to the CQA process:

"The Chairman's Quality Award process enables AT&T business units and divisions to check and compare their quality systems against the world-class criteria of the Baldrige Award. So we look at the Baldrige and the Chairman's Awards as the *check* step in the PDCA cycle," he says.

This PDCA-based process, then, starts out by performing the check, which gives the baseline. The check identifies companywide strengths as well as areas for improvement. In the check step, review rates of improvement and levels of participation are also reviewed. "The relative score comes out of the results of the Baldrige application criteria," says Myers.

"*Act* is the next step," he continues. "Here, recommendations from the feedback reports are reviewed, and priorities are set for Baldrige categories and initiatives. *Plan* is the third step. Here, strategic goals and targets for an improvement plan to meet the Baldrige criteria are set. The fourth step is the *do* step, where the support plans that were made to meet the Baldrige goals are implemented.

"That completes the PDCA cycle, but it keeps being repeated," Myers notes. "The cycle is continued because we do the check again so that we'll know how well we are doing—whether we are going off in the right direction or need to readjust our plans. Then once more, we move through the other steps."

VOLUNTARY PARTICIPATION ENCOURAGES CQA PROCESS SUCCESS

"In 1990, 23 business units and divisions participated in the Chairman's Award process," Myers reports. "They had received a challenge to measure themselves against world-class criteria and to develop strategies for significant, continuous improvement. However, they were not *ordered* to do so.

"Participation in the Chairman's Quality Award Process is *voluntary*; it is not *dictated*," Myers stresses. This is important for the following reason, he suggests: When top management *mandates* improvement, only a half-hearted response generally follows. People do what they are told only because it is *required* of them, so they don't do a very good job. As a result, they don't benefit from it, and top management doesn't get meaningful information from them. "So mandatory programs don't do anybody any good," he notes.

"This process will only be important as long as people feel it is useful to them. Our program has been based solely on its perceived value. So when I say our business participation—which was completely voluntary—went from 50 percent last year to 85 percent this year, that's a significant fact: It means that the business units perceive that the process is valuable to them," Myers points out.

"So far, we have been encouraging the business units to participate on an annual basis." he adds. (The CQA Process is an annual program.) Myers suggests that some people at AT&T believe that every *other* year would be fine, because they need time after they receive their feedback to work on implementing suggested improvements. However, he points out, everyone is required to do *business* and *financial* plans annually. "Since customer satisfaction is a key element to success in the marketplace, then [quality improvement plans] should be managed the same way [as business and financial plans]. So up to this point, we have encouraged annual participation."

A NEW PARADIGM TO ANALYZE THE BUSINESS AND SERVE THE CUSTOMER

"Until 1984, AT&T was a monopoly; it wasn't driven by the customer," Myers concedes. "The consequence of this environment is that we had a large number of managers and an infrastructure that were not driven by external customer requirements, and were inexperienced at competing in the marketplace.

"The philosophy of AT&T's redirection in November 1988 was to place responsibility and accountability for business operation in the hands of the business units," he explains. "Based on this philosophy, we do not have corporate programs for supplier and customer management. However, business units have a supplier management program and approach to identify customer requirements and evaluate their satisfaction.

"Many business units have formed quality improvement teams with the key customers and/or suppliers," Myers continues. "For example, we recently sponsored a 'sharing rally' focused on supplier management. The objective was to bring together all the key influencers for supplier management in all the business units. We brought the key person in each unit who is involved with supplier management and purchases to the rally to put together an AT&T supplier policy, and also to develop the support infrastructure to manage it. So we are moving toward a more aggressive, vigorous AT&T Supplier Management Program."

Of course, the more "vigorously" AT&T manages its suppliers—and its overall operations—the more effectively it can assure quality throughout its organization and then out to its external customers. "The Baldrige criteria and the CQA process have given us a new paradigm to analyze the business," Myers stresses. "It shows us how we are managing and running our operations from the customer's point of view.

"The award process is a useful mechanism for getting people to think about how to better satisfy their customers. Think of the award application as a mirror that you can hold up and reflect back to management. You may have a picture in your mind of how you are running your business, but when you look in that mirror, you see how you are *really* running the business in terms of meeting the needs of external customers."

FMC Corporation

To gain optimum benefit from the Baldrige criteria, this company has designed a comprehensive Baldrige-based self-appraisal matrix, which you can "customize" to realize improvement in *your* operation.

Like many companies, FMC Corporation (Chicago) was in search of an effective methodology to train its people in world-class quality practices. The company also needed a measurement process that would allow the corporate level as well as the operating unit level (groups, divisions, and sites) to determine where they needed to focus their improvement efforts.

The search led FMC to the criteria for the Malcolm Baldrige National Quality Award, which was first introduced to the company in 1988. "In time, we were able to show top management that the Baldrige criteria were legitimate tools for improving performance," says Stan David, corporate director of Quality.

Award Winning Quality

"The only problem was that we didn't have the logistical capabilities to complete 77-page applications for 30 divisions and 90-plus operations."

To overcome this hurdle, FMC came up with a Baldrige-based Total Quality Excellence Self-Appraisal Matrix (see Figure 6-1). The matrix is a methodology designed to accomplish these two basic goals:

① *To help management teams at the division and site levels to better understand what the Baldrige criteria mean and what is expected of them under the world-class model*

② *To help management teams evaluate themselves with respect to the model and gain an understanding of where they are and what areas need improvement*

FMC's TQE matrix is made up of the same seven "sections" as are the Baldrige criteria: Leadership, Human Resources Utilization, Strategic Quality Planning, Information and Analysis, Quality Assurance of Products and Services, Quality Results, and Customer Satisfaction. However, because quality assurance of products and services refers to separate aspects of FMC's business, the company created two columns for this in its matrix: Product Assurance System and Non-Product Assurance System. FMC then added two additional columns, Customer Satisfaction Measurement and Measurement of Improvement, to bring more attention to these areas.

Overall, the FMC matrix "explodes" the specific Baldrige questions into definitive statements about the following two issues:

⇨ *Whether certain management elements exist*
⇨ *Whether there is an approach, deployment, and result similar to the Baldrige grading system*

The statements in each box in the matrix correspond to questions in the Baldrige examination, and are referenced in a guide that goes along with the matrix. Each criterion is analyzed individually and ranked with the focus on identifying a total organizational baseline from which improvements can be measured.

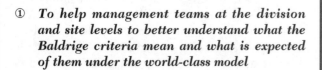

"The key to success in working across the columns is to maintain a balance between _technical_ improvements and _people_ improvements. There must be a blend of both. Too much of one and not enough of the other will not lead to success."

"Each year, we redo the matrix in line with any Baldrige criteria changes so that we can keep it current," reports David. However, other changes are limited; the goal is to keep it as consistent as possible in order to ensure stability and common understanding throughout the organization.

USING THE MATRIX FOR QUALITY IMPROVEMENT

At least once a year, every operation within FMC is encouraged to conduct a self-assessment using the matrix. The effort is designed to take no more than six to eight hours (although many operations choose to spend more time on the process).

"Each operation looks at itself area by area, criterion by criterion, to assess how well it is really doing," *continued on page 104*

Total Quality Excellence Self-Appraisal Matrix

Rate your appraisal (0-4) of each criteria in the Matrix using the definitions at right.

	0	1	2	3	4
Columns 1 - 7	None/Isolated	Minimum	Adequate	Fully Met	World Class
Column 8	Not Acceptable	Declining but Acceptable	Level or Improving	Industry Leader	Worldwide Leader
Column 9	Lagging Behind Competition	Matching Competition	Slightly Leading Competition	Strongly Leading Competition	World Class

1. LEADERSHIP	2. HUMAN RESOURCES	3. QUALITY STRATEGIC PLANNING	4. INFORMATION AND ANALYSIS	5. PRODUCT ASSURANCE SYSTEM	6. NON-PRODUCT ASSURANCE SYSTEM	7. CUSTOMER SATISFACTION MEASUREMENT SYSTEMS	8. MEASUREMENT OF IMPROVEMENT	9. CUSTOMER SATISFACTION
Verbal Q Support	Employee Well-Being and Morale	Qualitative Operational Q Improvement Goals Exist	Employee-Related Data Collection and Analysis	Safety, Health, and Environment Compliance/ Improvement System	Competitive Benchmarking System	Linkage of Customer Satisfaction to Outgoing Product Audit	Employee-Related Measures	Customer Satisfaction with the Products
Articulated Company Q Policy Promulgated/Communicated	Employees are Informed on Q Goals, Improvement Process	Quantitative Operational Q Improvement Goals Exist	Products/ Service/Process Data Collection and Analysis	Measurements/ Calibrations Standards Control System	Internal Customer/ Supplier Expectations Mapped	Linkage of Customer Satisfaction to Process Controls	Internal Service Measures	Customer Satisfaction with Delivery and Installation
Direct Executive Interaction with Multiple Levels	Q Improvement Training of All Employees	Functional Improvement Plan(s) Exist	Supplier Data and Analysis	Documentation Control System	Documentation Control System	Customer Service Standards	Internal Product Measures	Customer Satisfaction with Service and Maintenance
Mid and Local Level Manager Understanding/ Participation	Employees Inform Top Management on Q Goals, Improvement Process	Multifunctional Improvement Plan(s) Exist	Competitor Q Data and Analysis	Customer Input System for Existing Products	Customer Input System for Existing Services/ Non-Product Areas	Customer Satisfaction Measurement Systems for Guaranties and Warranties	Q Costs	Customer Satisfaction with Guaranties and Warranties
Well Defined Management Responsibilities/ Accountability for Q Improvement	Employees Identify/Resolve Q Issues	Periodic Correction to the Planning Process/Plan Progress	Distributor/ Dealer Data and Analysis	Customer Input System for New Products	Customer Input System for New Services/Non-Product Areas	Customer Satisfaction Measurement Systems for Complaint Handling Service	Complaints	Customer Satisfaction with Complaint Handling Service
Integration of Q Improvement with Management Structure	Staff Level Involvement in Q Improvement Process	Non-Management Employee Input into the Q Planning Process	Customer Data and Analysis	Interdepartment Input System for New Products	Interdepartment Input System for New Services/ Non-Product Areas	Customer Satisfaction Measurement Systems for the Complaint Level	Other Claims/ Recalls/ Litigation	Customer Satisfaction with the Complaint Level
Interdepartmental Improvement/ Prevention Activities	Degree of Employee Involvement in Q Improvement Process	Supplier Input into the Q Planning Process	Use of Standard Statistical Methods	Specific Q Improvement Objectives for Existing Products	Specific Q Improvement Objectives for Existing Services/ Non-Product Areas	Customer Satisfaction Measurement Systems for Delivery	Warranty Claims	Customer Satisfaction with Price and Value
Business-Wide Quality Improvement Structure	Recognition of Employee Q Improvement Contributions	Customer Input into Q Planning Process	Formal Q Information Feedback	Specific Q Improvement Objectives for New Products	Specific Q Improvement Objectives for New Services/ Non-Product Areas	Customer Satisfaction Measurement Systems for Price	External Assessments	
Q Improvement Resource Allocation/ Buffering	Real Time Recognition/ Compensation	Integration of Q Improvement Plans with Business Plans	Linkage of Analysis to Corrective Action	Assurance/ Validation System	Assurance/ Validation System	Customer Satisfaction Measurement Systems for Competitive Status of Prods. and Services	Market Share	
Public Responsibility/ Communication Activities	Q Improvement Essential Elements of Promotion/ Personnel System	Q Improvement Process which Attains/ Maintains World Class Position	Integrated Application of Information Technology	Product Assurance System Audited	Non-Product Assurance System Audited		Profitability	
Total	Total	Total	Total	Total	Total	Total	Total	Total

Figure 6-1: Baldrige Self-Assessment Matrix

continued from page 102

says David. "There are a lot of deliberations and a lot of discussions, which we encourage; this is part of the learning process."

To begin, a "diagonal slice" of the organization forms a review team. Each member of the review team at the operation studies the matrix and identifies the statements that he or she feels accurately represent what is occurring in the operation.

Next, the members meet in a joint session and form a consensus score for each criterion on the matrix while reviewing the results for implications and strategy development. Once they have this overall view of how their operation is doing, they develop action plans for improvement. In time, as the action plans are implemented, the team again reviews the matrix and develops new action plans.

"The key to success in working across the columns is to maintain a balance between *technical* improvements and *people* improvements," maintains David. "There must be a blend of both. Too much of one and not enough of the other will not lead to success."

THE ULTIMATE GOAL: BETTER CUSTOMER SERVICE

The ultimate goal of FMC's TQE process is to better serve its customers. At the same time, however, a number of operations are working toward entering the Baldrige competition.

"Current and past successes related to improvement are having a positive impact on the rest of the organization," notes David. In fact, as operations improve, they build appetites for new methodologies that can help them improve even more. "We sometimes have a hard time in the corporate quality office keeping up with the demand for education, training, and other support material."

One thing that David and his quality staffers *do* keep up with is an annual study of all of the company's operations as they relate to the matrix. The study has revealed numerous successes, such as the following:

★ The Fuels Control Division, which makes connectors for the oil industry, launched a TQE drive several years ago with a focus on cycle time reduction. In 1988-89, it began benchmarking itself against its competition to identify opportunities for improvement. By 1989-1990, the division had implemented cellular manufacturing, a decentralized structure, a total preventive maintenance system, and supplier management, all of which led to improvements management never thought possible.

★ The Ground Systems Division (GSD) of the Defense Group, which builds the Bradley fighting vehicle for the U.S. Army, implemented TQE as a way to become proactive with its customer. "Prior to this, GSD had been strictly reactive to MIL-Standard 9858-A," explains David. But the division began training in SPC, problem-solving, communications, work simplification, and process management.

"Within a year, the division had created a partnership with the Army on proactive quality improvements. This is significantly improving our performance and continuously making a good product better for our ultimate customers: the troops in the field."

Granite Rock

To make critical improvements in your company's processes, you must first *define* those processes—and then define what quality means for each one. The Baldrige criteria are helping this forward-thinking organization to do just that—year after year.

"We use the Baldrige application for continuous quality improvement," asserts Dave Franceschi, manager of Quality Support at Granite Rock (Watsonville, CA), a "high-end" building materials supplier. Granite Rock mines aggregate, sells building materials, makes and delivers ready-mixed concrete, and produces asphalt.

"For Granite Rock, the Baldrige is an internal self-improvement tool," explains Franceschi. "We believe in continuous improvement—we believed in it *before* the Baldrige even existed.

"Self-evaluation—which is what the process forces you to do—produces innovation, which in turn produces improved processes. In our 'World Economy,' the competition affects everyone. A business can survive only through improvement. The Baldrige forces you to stay on your toes."

Granite Rock goes through extensive information-gathering in preparation for the Baldrige Award application process. "We have approximately 20 branches and locations. These individual locations gather their own information, including customer satisfaction information from surveys (see box for more information on Granite Rock's customer-survey system), and information on on-time delivery and plant uptime," he explains.

> **"A business can survive only through improvement. The Baldrige forces you to stay on your toes."**

"We require our division managers to choose about half a dozen key areas—areas that can make or break their businesses—to measure and track. All the information they gather is sent to the Quality Support Department, which consists of me and my part-time boss, who came out of retirement to coordinate the application effort.

"It takes both of us four to six months to compile the data and write the application. This information is flowing into our department continuously." Franceschi adds that the company is now building information-gathering devices into its operations. And as a result, the Baldrige application process is becoming more manageable each year.

"We've applied for the Award every year since 1989," he notes. In 1991, the company received a site visit.

HARD DATA HELP FOCUS AND CLARIFY QUALITY

As any company that has applied for the Baldrige Award knows, the application process clearly involves painstaking work. Why does Granite Rock go through the paces year after year? According to Franceschi, the primary reason is that doing so helps provide focus and definition with regard to critical areas.

"The application is a real brain-buster—I think anyone reading it for the first time would agree," he concedes. "It's a new language for most people, and it requires considerable study."

Award Winning Quality

But the work is well worth the effort: "The Baldrige process has helped us to determine some of the areas we needed to measure," Franceschi asserts. "If you can't measure a process or function, you can't control it. The Baldrige focuses you to manage *by fact*, something that everyone *thinks* they do until they are actually asked for the hard data.

"With the Baldrige, you are asked to verify—with hard, factual data—how your strategic plans are implemented and tracked, what quality assurance techniques you've used, what results you've achieved using these techniques, and finally, how all of this has affected customer satisfaction. The hard data we've acquired with the help of the Baldrige have influenced our managerial decisions dramatically. It has helped us focus our efforts," reports Franceschi.

"Quality is a confusing issue unless you focus on the critical areas. The application leads you through seven categories—from leadership to customer satisfaction. It's a blueprint for improving all the quality aspects of a company."

THE BENEFITS OF A "BEAUTIFUL SYSTEM"

According to Franceschi, the Baldrige process is "a beautiful system. I think companies that take it seriously, use it primarily as a tool for improvement, and work hard will reap tremendous benefits in a short period of time." Here, he says, are some of those benefits:

> "It's a beautiful system. I think companies that take it seriously, use it primarily as a tool for improvement, and work hard will reap tremendous benefits in a short period of time."

➤ **Better definition of individual processes.** "Defining a 'process' is a key element to quality improvement," he stresses. "If you are the United States Mint and you're having problems with the penny-making machine, you must focus your attention on the penny-making process *only*. By focusing, you'll improve the process at a much faster rate."

➤ **Clarifying what quality means.** "We use the Baldrige for clarity," Franceschi says. "Quality is a confusing concept. A *quality* automobile is a good example. To buyers who require room for two kids and a dog, and who take lots of vacations, a quality automobile is a fuel-efficient station wagon or minivan. On the other hand, for a single adult who wants to drive fast, a quality automobile might be a Corvette.

"People talk about quality, but they really don't know what it means," Franceschi continues. "I believe the word 'quality' has been overused and abused. After completing the Baldrige application, terms like 'Big Q' or 'Total Quality' become clearer—the fog begins to lift. The more you participate [in the Baldrige process], the clearer 'quality' becomes.

"The Baldrige process forces you to define quality and to measure it accordingly. With a definition in hand, you eliminate the gray area: You either have it or you *don't*. Once you know where you are regarding quality, you can make decisions about where you want to be."

➤ **Enhanced benchmarking capability.** Accord-

ing to Franceschi, benchmarking is a highly effective way to help bring focus to your processes. What types of benchmarking does Granite Rock do? "Lots—both internal and external," replies Franceschi. "We're looking everywhere [for best practices that we can learn from].

"We've had little luck with our competitors. The construction industry is one of the oldest and largest industries in the United States. We've been unable to find competitors or others in the business that are doing the things we are.

"Our co-CEO Bruce W. Woolpert—who along with his brother Steve took over operation from their parents several years ago—brought many progressive ideas to the company. We're finding that our direct competitors—and very few companies in our industry—are as progressive as we are. Therefore, we're forced to go outside the industry to benchmark other companies' processes."

IMPROVEMENT—NOT WINNING— IS THE PRIMARY GOAL

"Some of the Award winners have used the Baldrige process to rebound from difficult times, but that's not the reason we've applied," Franceschi points out. "Granite Rock is 90 years old and has been strong for many years. We chose to compete for *self-improvement*. And we *are* getting stronger with the help of the Baldrige process.

"For example, both our financial results and our customer satisfaction ratings have been more positive," he reports. "Customers tell us that on-time delivery (OTD) is their top priority, and our OTD tracking shows continuous improvement. Our customers tell us they are happy, and in a declining market, our market share is increasing.

"We expect to win the Baldrige soon," Franceschi asserts. "And when we do, it will be a pat on the back for everyone who makes the company work. But even after we *do* win, we still plan to continue completing the criteria each year.

"Our main goal in going through the Baldrige application process isn't to win, but to improve the company," he stresses. "We believe the main purpose of the application is for in-house reevaluation and improvement. It's more important to share that information within the company than to win the Award. The Baldrige application process is only one of the tools we use to support quality improvement throughout Granite Rock."

A Customer Feedback System That Really Makes the Grade

Surveying customers helps you to ascertain exactly what they want and need from your organization in the way of quality. Once you have determined this, you can make customer-pleasing improvements throughout your organization.

To accomplish this, Granite Rock sends detailed and extensive surveys to both established and prospective customers every three to five years. These customers are asked to rank in order—from most to least important—what they consider critical characteristics in a supplier.

As a follow-up to this survey, the company conducts less detailed surveys of its current and potential customer base each year. The questions in this survey are geared toward determining how customers rank Granite Rock's performance in comparison with that of the other suppliers they use. Customers can grade Granite Rock and its competitors from "A" for "the best" through "F" for "terrible." While the first survey focuses on determining which areas customers consider important, this follow-up survey asks customers to rate Granite Rock's performance in each of those areas. Although the two types of surveys differ in the frequency with which they are administered, in their length, and in their purpose, they do have three things in common:

➤ **Approximately 25 percent of the space in both surveys is devoted to *open-ended* questions.** The responses customers give to these types of questions provide the clearest idea of what is on their minds.

➤ **Both surveys are eye-pleasing and easy to complete.** Customers tend to ignore surveys that are difficult to fill out or take a long time to complete.

➤ **Both surveys may be sent out again if customers fail to return them.** Sometimes an added incentive—such as a dollar bill for a cup of coffee—is sent along with the survey.

SHARE SURVEY INFO WITH ALL STAFFERS

Keep in mind that surveys alone aren't effective unless you convey to all staffers at your company the information that customers share. That way, *they'll* know just how customers feel about the work they do, and they'll be able to determine what steps they need to take to keep those customers satisfied.

Each year, management at Granite Rock analyzes the results of its surveys, charts them in an easy-to-read format, and posts the resulting grids on the employee bulletin boards at each branch office location. Each grid compares Granite Rock's performance with that of a competitor.

The *vertical* axis addresses results from the three- to five-year surveys that determine what customers consider important. The *horizontal* axis addresses results from the annual surveys that determine how customers rank Granite Rock's performance. Points are awarded on this axis for customer grades of "A" or "B." Each of the four resulting quadrants has a significant meaning:

➡ *Strengths*, the *top right* quadrant, identifies factors that customers consider important and at which they believe supplier performance excels.

➡ *Vulnerabilities*, the *top left* quadrant, identifies factors that customers consider important, and they feel that supplier performance is lacking in these areas.

➡ *No One Cares*, the *bottom left* quadrant, identifies factors that customers consider unimportant but they feel that supplier performance is lacking in these areas.

➡ *Nice to Have*, the *bottom right* quadrant, identifies factors that customers consider unimportant, but they nonetheless feel that supplier performance excels in these areas.

While Granite Rock is pleased when a large number of factors fall into the upper right quadrant, it is concerned with how this compares with its competitors' scores: If just as many of the competitors' scores fall into this same quadrant, then the company knows it has some work to do if it wants to move even further ahead of its rivals in the marketplace. So the final step is to take the information on the grids and determine what changes and improvements need to be made. These remedial actions can take two forms:

➲ **Resolving individual problems with specific customers.** Customers may either return their surveys anonymously or identify themselves. Each option has advantages: Anonymity allows customers the freedom to be candid; when they identify themselves, Granite Rock has a chance to provide personalized assistance.

➲ **Resolving pervasive problems identified by a number of customers.** These can fall under either Vulnerabilities or Strengths (but competitors are doing equally well in those areas). Teams are formed to address these issues and come up with improvement plans to make sure customers are never troubled by these problems again.

Inland Steel Bar Company

This company uses the Baldrige criteria as a benchmarking tool for continuous improvement; to gain the feedback it needs to gauge progress toward quality goals and determine where improvement is still needed.

When Inland Steel Bar Company (East Chicago, IN) was spun off from Inland Steel Company in 1988, management made a conscious effort to create a different kind of organization. "We wanted to be more responsive to our customers and our market," explains Alan Wilgus, manager of Human Resources. "We also wanted to create a lean organization that utilized a work team structure."

In working toward world-class supplier status, management also realized that it must fall in line with the criteria that firmly establish other world-class suppliers. "We did a lot of benchmarking in terms of who were the people in our business who were truly successful," states Wilgus. "We wanted to find out what differentiated them from everyone else."

It quickly became obvious to management that pursuing the Baldrige criteria was one of the major ways the company could benchmark itself and seek long-term continuous improvement.

Award Winning Quality

THREE QUALITY INITIATIVES FOR CONTINUOUS IMPROVEMENT

The effort first began in the company's quality department. "We had a good quality system in place," points out Wilgus. "However, after studying the Baldrige criteria, we realized that we fell short in some areas.

"In addition, we realized that we didn't have a strong link between all the criteria. Our quality initiatives were somewhat fragmented."

In beginning to move toward consistent Baldrige-level excellence, the company created three important initiatives:

■ **Quality Council.** This consists primarily of members of the company's management team (the president and his direct reports). "The council's role is patterned after what Juran calls a process for continuous improvement," states Wilgus.

The council directs initiatives that are designed to solve what have been identified as critical quality problems. "We have instituted standardized procedures designed to guide process improvement," he

continues. This is the Plan-Do-Check-Act (PDCA) cycle (see section on AT&T, also in this chapter). "We also encourage team involvement as part of the effort," he adds.

> **"The Baldrige provides excellent feedback on where we are in our journey and where we still need to go."**

The program is monitored through monthly presentations by the teams, which report their progress.

■ **Cost of Quality.** Management has also embraced the importance of understanding the cost of quality. "This is the amount it costs us in terms of waste and rework," states Wilgus. "It also addresses positive costs of quality, such as cost avoidance from equipment breakdowns through preventive maintenance." Cost of quality now drives business planning in the company.

■ **Organizational Restructuring.** The third initiative involves the way operating departments and staff departments interact. As much effort is being placed on improving quality in staff support functions as on improving quality in manufacturing.

"As an example, we are making a conscious effort to integrate activities across staff areas, rather than maintaining 'functional silos,'" continues Wilgus. (For an explanation of functional silos, see section on Motorola, Chapter Two.)

MEETING QUALITY CHALLENGES TODAY AND TOMORROW

Using Baldrige criteria as a way to assess oneself and make improvements is never an easy task. Wilgus identifies two of the challenges Inland Steel Bar faces in moving ahead:

"We are currently in the midst of a huge capital improvement program," he reports. "As a result, we are having to address some quality problems in an unstable environment." It is difficult to assess the impact of quality improvement efforts when the new equipment itself is still being brought under statistical process control. "It will be difficult to assess the total impact of our improvements until the new technology is under control," he notes.

> "Baldrige has a way of guiding your thinking. You can't go through the application process without thinking differently about the way you do business. It has been a very meaningful experience from this standpoint. Ultimately, the benefits will far outweigh the costs."

In addition, management realizes that implementing Baldrige criteria in an organization involves a cultural change. "It does not happen overnight, and it does not happen without a great deal of effort, persistence, and hard work," he emphasizes. "It represents a fundamental change in the way things are run."

THE BENEFITS ARE ALREADY EVIDENT

In spite of the challenges in its path, Inland Steel Bar has already seen some benefits to its Baldrige-based improvement efforts:

The company received preferred supplier status from both General Motors Corporation (through Mark of Excellence) and Ford Motor Company (through Q-1), the first steel company to receive such recognition from both automakers. The company also received certified supplier status from Caterpillar Inc.

Applying for the Baldrige Award in 1990, Inland Steel Bar finished in the top 22 percent, just missing the cutoff for a site visit. However, the feedback it received from the examiners proved extremely valuable in making more improvements. "The Baldrige provides excellent feedback on where we are in our journey and where we still need to go," reports Wilgus.

"Baldrige has a way of guiding your thinking. You can't go through the application process without thinking differently about the way you do business. It has been a very meaningful experience from this standpoint.

"Ultimately, the benefits will far outweigh the costs, and this will be the only way to go," Wilgus concludes.

Intel Corporation

This Baldrige Award finalist is using the application process to help assure a strong position in a fiercely competitive market.

It's no secret that electronics is one of the most competitive industries in the world today. That makes it a challenge for electronics companies to build and maintain market share. However, it's an even greater challenge if you work for the most competitive division of a company involved in one of the most competitive areas of electronics.

This scenario well-defines the Semiconductor Products Group (SPG) of Intel Corporation (Chandler, AZ). SPG has been on a quality improvement mission since the mid-1980s. From this mission have sprung a number of successful efforts, explains Intel's Total Quality and Training Manager Scott Pfotenhauer.

Here's a look at Intel's quality plan, and how the Baldrige process fits into that plan.

Award Winning Quality

AN OVERVIEW OF INTEL'S QUALITY PROCESS

According to Pfotenhauer, Intel's quality strategy consists of the following elements:

■ **Quality Improvement Process.** This problem-solving strategy helps management identify opportunities for improvement and implement the necessary changes. Teams of employees are assigned to address each area of improvement, using customer requirements and world-class performance as their guidelines. Solutions that prove successful are standardized to ensure continuity.

■ **Management for Values Program.** This program is designed to coordinate Intel's goals with values based on work ethic, risk-taking, and customer orientation. Key to the success of this effort is extensive quality training and employee empowerment.

■ **Supplier Continuous Quality Improvement (SCQI).** This effort involves partnering with suppliers and setting lofty but realistic performance goals for continuous improvement. Suppliers are evaluated on seven criteria:

❶ *Use of statistical process control*
❷ *Documentation*
❸ *Productivity improvement*
❹ *Leadership*

❺ *Total employee involvement*
❻ *Training*
❼ *Relationships with their suppliers*

"We have also used the SCQI criteria to assess *ourselves*," Pfotenhauer notes.

> **Those who win the IQA must demonstrate excellence in the area of continuous quality improvement, based on Baldrige criteria and Intel corporate values.**

■ **Vendor of Choice (VOC) System.** This effort is designed to gather information from customers on what they consider to be important for their suppliers, such as Intel. The company's survey asks customers to rank it in the areas of *service, technology, price, delivery,* and *quality.* A follow-up survey then asks the customers to rank Intel in comparison to its competitors.

➤ *VOC in Action* ➤ Pfotenhauer cites an example of VOC in action. "In 1988, we began an effort to earn Ford Motor Company's Total Quality Excellence Award," he states. TQE involves a broad assessment of suppliers that support Ford. "Using Ford's 80 to 90 different criteria, we assessed ourselves," Pfotenhauer explains. "Then Ford assessed us." The exercise helped SPG understand its areas of strength and weakness, then to create appropriate improvement plans. SPG won Ford's TQE in 1990. To date, only five other suppliers have won the prestigious award.

RESPONDING TO CUSTOMER FEEDBACK LEADS TO QUALITY AWARD

In response to the customer feedback it has gained through VOC, Intel has launched a number of efforts. Among them are the following:

➤ **Perfect Design Quality, Pretty Darn Quick (PDQ, PDQ) Program:** This helps Intel bring products to market more quickly by improving communication between design teams and encouraging more parallel development of products.

➤ **Management by Planning (MBP):** This is a fusing of management tools, data-gathering techniques, and close tracking of plans in order to respond to feedback from VOC, "culture audits," and employee suggestions.

➤ **Quality Function Deployment (QFD):** This is a support function for MBP that seeks specific customer input on product design requirements.

CREATING A "BALDRIGE CLIMATE": SELF-ASSESSMENT AND INTERNAL AWARD

In spite of all these efforts and resulting successes, SPG still found itself unable to locate a comprehensive measurement system by which it could track its own performance and set goals for future improvements. Then along came the Malcolm Baldrige National Quality Award in 1987. "Baldrige is a comprehensive self-assessment tool that almost everyone recognizes and accepts," explains Pfotenhauer. "By using it, we are now able to generate a lot of valuable feedback."

To create a Baldrige "climate" within the organization, Intel created the Intel Quality Award (IQA). The IQA is bestowed each year to only one executive staff level group within the company and up to three organizations from within that group. Those who win the IQA must demonstrate excellence in the area of continuous quality improvement, based on Baldrige criteria and Intel corporate values.

Entrants must complete the Baldrige self-assessment and prove that they could attain at least 500 points out of a possible 1,000 points on the Baldrige exam.

Those who qualify then advance to the next step, in which they show how they exemplify Intel's six corporate values, which are

★ **Results orientation**
★ **Risk-taking**
★ **Discipline**
★ **Customer satisfaction**
★ **Quality**
★ **Assuring a "great place to work"**

The applications are reviewed by senior management and then forwarded to three senior executives for final selection.

> "In the future, Intel will take the lessons learned from its Semiconductor Products Group and proliferate them across the company. They believe they will become more competitive, efficient, and better able to serve their customers."

REACHING FOR THE BALDRIGE MEANS SERVING CUSTOMERS BETTER

Besides using Baldrige criteria as a way to make continuous improvements, SPG is seeking to go a step further and win the Award. In fact, SPG is the first Intel division to actually apply for the Baldrige.

During its first attempt, in 1990, the Group assembled over 100 representatives to become a self-assessment team. The team then spent over 10,000 hours on the self-assessment process. The effort was well worth it, in that SPG was named as a finalist and received a site visit by Baldrige examiners.

Using the Baldrige feedback and "post mortem" from 1990, SPG teams highlighted some of the areas that needed improvement, and set to work on them. SPG then applied again in 1991, and received another site visit.

"In the future, Intel will take the lessons learned from its Semiconductor Products Group and proliferate them across the company," says Pfotenhauer. "They believe they will become more competitive, efficient, and better able to serve their customers."

Pall Corporation

Benchmarking itself against the Baldrige criteria was one step toward this already excellent company's development of its Total Quality Performance process and Customer Satisfaction Program.

Pall Corporation (East Hills, NY) is the world leader in design, production, and marketing of fine filters and other fluid clarification devices. Pall's products are used to remove solid, liquid, or gaseous contaminants from liquids and gases, in a wide variety of applications in three primary markets: Healthcare, Aeropower, and Fluid Processing. Although already an industry leader, Pall has implemented a total quality process and is working toward becoming even stronger. The Baldrige criteria are a tool the company is using to this end.

"We began formal planning for total quality management systems throughout Pall Corporation in the autumn of 1989," reports Patricia J. Iannucci, vice president of Marketing Services at Pall's Corporate Headquarters. "Our initial focus was to be on our North American operations, which involves some 3,500 people," she explains.

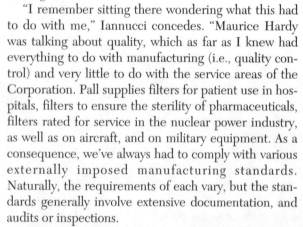

Award Winning Quality

"At that time, our CEO, Maurice G. Hardy, had a meeting with a variety of managers, during which he announced his intention to implement Total Quality Management, and ultimately, to compete for the Malcolm Baldrige Award.

"I remember sitting there wondering what this had to do with me," Iannucci concedes. "Maurice Hardy was talking about quality, which as far as I knew had everything to do with manufacturing (i.e., quality control) and very little to do with the service areas of the Corporation. Pall supplies filters for patient use in hospitals, filters to ensure the sterility of pharmaceuticals, filters rated for service in the nuclear power industry, as well as on aircraft, and on military equipment. As a consequence, we've always had to comply with various externally imposed manufacturing standards. Naturally, the requirements of each vary, but the standards generally involve extensive documentation, and audits or inspections.

"In fact, I couldn't help but wonder why Pall needed [to implement TQM and participate in the Baldrige process] at all," she admits. "After all, our founder, Dr. David B. Pall, had been nominated for—and ultimately received—the National Medal of Technology, we were a strong contender for the Fortune 500, which we subsequently made, and our sales and earnings reported record growth year after year."

However, this already excellent company saw a way to become even *better*, and it wasn't about to pass up the chance for further improvement.

AN OPPORTUNITY TO BECOME EVEN BETTER

"Again, it was during this initial quality meeting that we were told that we would ultimately compete for the Baldrige Award—the only question was one of timing," Iannucci recalls. "This was prompted by a customer's urging that all its suppliers do so.

"We're fortunate to have a diverse, worldwide customer base—we didn't have to take on this task to keep one customer. However, the opportunity was there and our management saw it," she notes.

This opportunity for improvement would help Pall to keep the cost of quality down and make itself an even more desirable supplier in the eyes of its customers. "Companies that had bought into the Total Quality Management philosophy would ultimately require the same of their suppliers," Iannucci notes. "It made perfect sense: Suppliers that make mistakes are expensive to do business with.

"Customers are justifiably concerned with the total cost of doing business. Product, price, and performance are large factors. Suppliers that don't ship on time, have high rework rates, and make shipping and billing errors cost them money.

"We're seeing more and more companies expressing a strong willingness to work together with their suppliers to help them meet requirements," Iannucci continues. "These companies then reward those suppliers that meet their requirements with more of their business. And they aren't shy to point out that those suppliers that aren't serious about continuous quality improvement will ultimately be dropped!"

LEARNING SOME EARLY LESSONS ABOUT TOTAL QUALITY

"Following that first quality meeting, I voraciously read everything that related to Total Quality Management (as opposed to quality control) that I could get my hands on," says Iannucci. "I learned that quality was as much the responsibility of the sales, marketing, and services departments as it was the manufacturing department's.

"In fact, although Manufacturing was the traditional scapegoat of quality problems, research shows that Manufacturing is only culpable for 30 percent of them," she notes. "Rework, errors, missed deadlines, the results of poor communication, run rampant throughout most organizations, but they are not tracked and measured as they are in a manufacturing environment. Yet, they all influence product and service quality, and add to costs.

"The quality gurus (Crosby, Deming, Juran, etc.) preached that poor quality costs a company as much as 25 percent of sales. Through Total Quality Management, these costs could be systematically identified, analyzed, and eliminated. Practitioners of Total Quality Management gave glowing testimony to Total Quality Management, which they regarded as their savior. Industry leaders warned that American industry needed Total Quality Management to compete with competitors that had become world class."

FIRST BALDRIGE AUDIT REVEALED AREAS NEEDING IMPROVEMENT

"Our vice president, Quality Assurance and Regulatory Affairs department had served on the Board of Directors of the American Society for Quality Control (ASQC) when the Baldrige Award criteria were developed. He arranged for each of our facilities to audit itself against the Baldrige criteria in the Spring of 1990," reports Iannucci.

"The application was used to focus interviews within different areas of the organization. All seven sections of Baldrige criteria were covered in interviews with department heads, supervisors, and line employees. This resulted in a written report with various recommendations for improvement."

> "Companies today have learned that the quality of their products and services must be superb, and that they can't dictate terms to customers anymore. The customer really is king."

"We compared ourselves department by department against the Baldrige criteria. In a few areas, wide gaps emerged, but we weren't bothered by this. The Award categories gave us a way to focus our improvement efforts. Thirty percent of the scoring on the Baldrige application is related to customer service. The application asks questions about how you interact with your customers. Do you solicit their ideas, ask them whether you are giving them what they want, the way they want it, when they want it, and how they want it? If you don't do this, you don't have any score.

"We have never thought of the Baldrige just as a prize," Iannucci stresses. "We're not involved in the process to win prizes or ribbons. Our goal is *continuous improvement*. It is a system—to which all of us are committed—of continually establishing higher requirements, measuring our progress toward them, and constantly identifying and correcting the underlying causes of any deviations from our goals.

"We benchmarked ourselves against the Baldrige criteria and had not done very well in some areas. So we set it aside for the time being. Then we began outlining some of our objectives and developing strategies to achieve them."

BALDRIGE APPLICATION LEADS TO TOTAL QUALITY PERFORMANCE

Pall Corporation recognized the fact that getting all staffers behind the quality effort was absolutely critical to achieving total, Baldrige-level quality. "We realized that a lot of our success would hinge upon raising all our employees' awareness, getting them to support us, and then training them so that they'd be able to respond. This is why we call our total quality management process 'Total Quality Performance'; the emphasis is not on management alone," Iannucci explains.

"Our top executives went through their initial quality training in the Summer of 1990. Their subordinates followed immediately thereafter; then we made plans to train the rest of the work force within two years."

Communicating the company's quality goals to all employees was a necessary prerequisite to initiating their training. "Before we began to train the majority of employees, we introduced our first companywide newsletter," Iannucci says. "This publication would be our primary communication vehicle (outside of formal and informal meetings at the plant level) to raise awareness and instill worker pride in the corporation."

Content in the newsletter is carefully orchestrated to achieve the following quality goals:

★ **To educate employees about the company and quality**
★ **To help spread and preserve the company's revered culture**
★ **To report on progress within the Total Quality Performance process**
★ **To inspire and motivate employees to do a better job tomorrow than they did today**

Trained management groups formed improvement teams and began designing a structure so that employees could participate. They subsequently began to identify problems that they plan to address.

"During our first year, we trained more than 60

percent of our North American staff. Many of the requisite quality systems are now in place, improvement goals have been set, and workers are actively participating. We've unleashed an army of supporters who are using their new skills to eliminate problems," Iannucci reports.

"During the coming year, we will reaudit ourselves to gauge the progress we've made and to identify further areas for improvement."

SETTING REALISTIC GOALS FOR THE FUTURE

"Our management is looking forward to the efficiencies and overall improvements that will result from our quality process," says Iannucci. "However, we have been very careful to establish only realistic and achievable goals—particularly during our first year of implementation. After all, you can't ask untrained employees to participate. You'll only frustrate them.

"Now that most of our employees are trained and many of our quality systems are in place, plant-level management is setting specific goals," she continues. "For example, one plant is looking toward making a 40 percent improvement in manufacturing cycle times within a given period. On a corporatewide basis over the next four years, we'd like to see a 25 percent reduction in the price of nonconformance—the enormous cost associated with doing things wrong or over.

"Since our objective is continuous improvement, once shorter-term goals have been met, we'll establish more stringent requirements," Iannucci adds.

DEVELOPING A PROGRAM TO SATISFY EVERY CUSTOMER

Pall began developing a Customer Satisfaction Program in 1991. The program is based on the premise that quality is driven and defined by the customer. The premise also required that Pall develop a proactive program that would first allow the company to survey its customers and determine their needs; and second, enable it to measure how effectively it was meeting those needs. The company defined its customer groups to include the following:

➤ **Distributors**
➤ **End users**
➤ **Customers with complaints**
➤ **Lost customers**
➤ **Prospects**
➤ **Those receiving special services**

Pall plans to use focus groups, mail surveys, phone interviews, and personal interviews to obtain customer feedback. The company also intends to ask customers to evaluate their overall satisfaction with their services, support, and products by providing feedback in seven key areas:

❶ **Overall business dealings**
❷ **Training, including practical applications**
❸ **Product literature**
❹ **Clinical applications of staff support**
❺ **Regional managers support**
❻ **Products**
❼ **Sales support**

Customers will be asked to evaluate such factors as product delivery time, product literature clarity and availability, and promptness of service. They will be also asked to rank each statement from one (very important) to ten (completely unimportant).

PUT THE CUSTOMER FIRST: A MATTER OF SURVIVAL

The bottom line when it comes to quality today is that the customers' needs must *always* come first, Iannucci stresses. And no company can afford to assume that it knows best what those needs are; it's crucial to get that information from your customers themselves. "There was an arrogance among leading-edge American companies before," she asserts. "They felt that they knew better than anyone what their customers wanted and what they would pay for. However, many of these companies fell on tough times—and some didn't survive.

"Companies today have learned that the quality of their products and services must be superb, and that they can't dictate terms to customers anymore. The customer really *is* king—it's an old line that everybody used and didn't really believe. However, anyone who doesn't believe it today—and demonstrates this by their actions—will find that they are on a one-way path to extinction," Iannucci points out.

She adds that the Baldrige is only one of the certifications that Pall is pursuing in its quest for top quality and total customer satisfaction. "Our European manufacturing plants are already registered in ISO 9000," she reports. "Ultimately, we believe that it's going to be a way to lock noncertified companies out of the European Economic Community. We believe that the same certification will become important in the U.S. as well, so we are working toward that here.

"All these various awards and certifications offer a great framework for looking at yourself in terms of how you serve your customer, how you treat your employees, what type of training you provide, what kind of turnover you have, as well as looking at the more traditional quality assurance of your products," Iannucci concludes.

The Perkin-Elmer Corporation

Setting more strategic business goals, improving benchmarking and teambuilding capabilities, and developing standardized reporting procedures are only a few of the many improvements this excellent organization has made through applying the Baldrige process.

The Perkin-Elmer Corporation (Norwalk, CT) is an international organization with manufacturing facilities in Europe as well as in the United States, and sales and service offices worldwide. The company is the global leader in instruments for chemical analysis, and employs 6,300 people.

Despite Perkin-Elmer's considerable size, management was determined to assure top quality not just in the manufacturing function, but across the board. "We started a quality program in 1984-85 that addressed quality at a global level and within *all* Perkin-Elmer departments—not solely in the manufacturing area," says Joseph E. Malandrakis, division vice president, North American Instrument Operations.

With such a large quality undertaking, it was clear that Perkin-Elmer needed a way to measure and track the success of its effort. The Baldrige process provided just the tool to accomplish that feat. "We are using the Baldrige application primarily to help self-assess the strengths of our internal quality process," Malandrakis explains. "What the Baldrige process has helped us do is to structure our quality process, highlighting such specific areas as employee involvement, communications, feedback, reports, and training. We also look at it as a way to get an independent outside group of quality experts to look at our operation and give us their appraisal of how well they think we're doing and what our strengths and weaknesses are."

FIRST TIME HELPS IMPROVE INTERNAL REPORTING PROCEDURES

Like many companies that have applied for the Baldrige Award over the course of a few years, Perkin-Elmer found the application process to be toughest the first year. "The first year was the most difficult for us," says Malandrakis. "We knew that our quality plan had been in effect since 1985, so our first application for the Baldrige was really to test the maturity of our plan and to benchmark ourselves against the world-class leaders who would also be applying for the Baldrige Award.

"We had eight people representing different functions of the corporation. It took these people several weeks—working about 10 to 20 hours a week—to put the application together. A lot of the time was spent fig-

uring out how to organize the report. They had to go out and collect the data from the teams that were in operation and then put it all together in an effective presentation. These were all time-consuming activities.

"The hardest part was assembling the data and putting the application together in the format the Baldrige examiners wanted to see," Malandrakis notes. "However, doing this helped us to better define the key elements of quality improvement, and then link our own internal processes with what the Baldrige assessed. This makes it easier for us to obtain the necessary information or feedback required for the Baldrige report.

"For example, in our operations we have many just-in-time teams, Achieving Competitive Excellence teams, and employee involvement teams that focus on product and process improvement. These teams are focused in specific areas, such as reducing waste, minimizing product development time, improving reliability, reducing lead and setup times—the entire gamut of productivity, efficiency, and quality measurements.

"These teams report their progress in formats that are key to our business planning, but that are also appropriate for presenting in the Baldrige application. So we can use the teams' reports to facilitate the data we need for the application, and eliminate some of the work that is normally involved,"

Award Winning Quality

> **"The Baldrige philosophy is helping us assess the critical things that we require to be competitive and to remain competitive. And it is continually stimulating us to set aggressive goals—and as we near those goals, to continuously challenge ourselves to do better."**

Malandrakis suggests. "We have standardized our internal reporting procedures, which also helps us to assemble data for the Baldrige application.

"Today, standardized forms for those reports are readily available in the organization," he adds. "We've organized our many internal teams and our own internal processes to present reports showing continuous process and product improvement."

EIGHT MORE GREAT BENEFITS THE BALDRIGE HAS BROUGHT

Besides helping Perkin-Elmer to standardize its internal reporting system, how else has the Baldrige process benefited the company? Here are eight of the primary improvements it has brought:

★ **More aggressive, strategic goal-setting.** "The entire Baldrige philosophy is helping us to assess the critical things that are required for us to be competitive and to remain competitive," says Malandrakis. "And more important, it is continually stimulating us to set aggressive goals—and as we near those aggressive goals, to continuously challenge ourselves to do better."

★ **Enhanced quality awareness.** "The application process has seriously helped our company understand what makes up the elements of quality, and to realize that it should not be focused in just one or two specific areas," Malandrakis asserts. "The application is really broad in scope and includes everyone from the customer right down to the person who is putting the product together.

"It's a more global deployment look at quality. It has really helped us in the overall awareness, in every level of the operation, of how critical quality is to the success of our corporation and to our ability to compete."

★ **Improved customer awareness.** "We surveyed our customers to find out what was important to them pertaining to the delivery and quality of the consumables that are used in our instrumentation," reports Malandrakis.

And not only are people at Perkin-Elmer becoming more aware of their customers' needs, customers are becoming more aware of the company's capabilities and commitment to excellence. "We share our quality efforts with our customers, so they are very much aware of our commitment, as evidenced by our participation in the Baldrige process.

"We include in our annual reports and other company literature the fact that we're going for the Baldrige and that we won the Connecticut Quality Improvement Award (an award that's based on the Baldrige). Recently, we have received inquiries concerning ISO 9000, and our current efforts will put us in a good position to meet this customer requirement

in the near future."

★ **Better benchmarking.** "We continued to recognize our need to poll our customers, but we also recognized the need to benchmark the 'best in class' of the distributors of consumer goods," explains Malandrakis. "This was one of the areas a few years back that we weren't that strong in, but we have come a long way. We benchmark with some of the previous winners of the Baldrige Award. We also use some of our key suppliers to benchmark against, as well as with. In addition, we look at competitive surveys.

"We recently hired a consultant who specializes in benchmarking," Malandrakis adds. "This consultant measured us and compared us against available data from the 'best in the class' type industries. We fared very well against these industries."

★ **Development of new, quality-driven operations.** "Based on the results of the customer polls and benchmarking of distributors, we created a new operating group in the company called PE Xpress (Perkin-Elmer Express)," Malandrakis reports. "PE Xpress provides training, supplies, and accessories via a catalog-type operation with a toll-free 800 hotline.

"While the Baldrige criteria didn't contribute entirely toward developing PE Xpress, it certainly reinforced our approach in organizing a new part of the business. It told us 'Let's take the specifics of customer satisfaction into valued consideration,' as well as the specifics of 'how to distribute goods to the customers.' We had to ask ourselves whether there was a better way of doing that, and we challenged ourselves to find that better way," continues Malandrakis. "That's why we went to a 'best in its class' distributor, benchmarked it, and got some good pointers.

"We measured other factors internally. We probably measured these even before the Baldrige process, so it was nice to confirm that what we were doing was considered essential to excel and to be world-class in such areas as lead time reduction, improved reliability, and faster response to our customers."

★ **Improved supplier management.** "When we won the Connecticut Award, our CEO issued a memo to all our suppliers telling them we had won this award, and that the Baldrige process is an excellent way of analyzing quality processes," Malandrakis recalls. "We encouraged them to apply for the Award, but we did not make it mandatory.

"We have stated that Perkin-Elmer will be doing business in the near future with companies that have a strong quality process, and who are familiar with just-in-time manufacturing and quality deployment. We stated via our internal just-in-time purchasing program that those are the companies that will be able to compete for our business. It will be an advantage if they are familiar with the Baldrige as well."

★ **Stronger employee participation and recognition.** "In 1989, we won the Connecticut Quality Improvement Award, which is modeled on the Baldrige application," says Malandrakis. "During that application process, we involved our employees in putting an application together.

"We shared the results with them and told them that we were to be audited. The audit team mingled with the employees to make sure our facts were accurate and the deployment was there from a vertical standpoint—that people not only understood there was a quality program here but understood that they were a part of that process.

"When we won the award, we put a banner up and had a recognition day. Our people know that we won the Connecticut Award, and that we're striving to win the Baldrige Award. They also realize that they have been a big part of making the Connecticut Award possible and that their help is continuing to make the Baldrige process successful for us."

★ **Problem-solving through teambuilding.** "We focus on employees and team building; all our improvements have been through a team cooperative effort," asserts Malandrakis. "These teams have spanned both product and process controls.

"For example, one new team was responsible for coming with a preferred parts list, which has helped us standardize the design and the development of our products. It's also helped us reduce the parts in all of our new products as much as 60 percent.

"We have another team in the electronics function that is focused on process improvement. This team has improved its first-pass test yields by over 35 percent.

"We have other teams that have focused on setup reductions, and they have achieved a better than 70 percent improvement," Malandrakis continues. "The lead times of all our instruments have benefited from setup reductions, improved first-pass yields, and lower quality defects. Also, lead times have been significantly reduced since we implemented the just-in-time process. Some lead times have been cut by as much as 50 to 60 percent on average, for all our instruments.

"Still other teams are active in such areas as product development and customer-related functions. This companywide team effort is a key driver in Perkin-Elmer being rated high in overall quality of products and services.

"We provide guidance to the teams through what we call an 'operations vision and architecture statement,' which primarily gives direction to all the groups within the company. It explains, for instance, what we mean when we say 'productivity and quality improvement,'" Malandrakis explains.

"As a part of that statement, we specifically give some examples of how we would like the information presented. A lot of that comes from internal meetings we have on the subject. But in any case, the data have to be presented in a format where the teams look at improvements quarter by quarter.

"For example, if a team is looking at first-pass test yields, we would like to see the actual reports, on a quarter-by-quarter basis, stating what their goals were, what the results were, what actions they put into place to achieve those results, and more important, how they are going to continue that positive trend."

To get this information back to the other levels of associates in the organization, Perkin-Elmer uses internal publications that are published on a quarterly basis. Communication is also accomplished through the teams that exist throughout the organization.

MAKING IMPROVEMENTS FOR SURVIVAL IN THE SPIRIT OF COOPERATION

"Our main goal in applying for the Baldrige Award is to use it as a vehicle to help us assess our overall performance in the areas of quality and productivity and to use it as a catalyst in promoting this process internally," Malandrakis asserts. "People here know that we applied for the Baldrige, that we scored high on it—we continue to score within the top 15 to 20 percent category—and that we're pleased with that.

"We understand that the improvements we are targeting aren't going to come about overnight, but we know that our internal processes are really keyed in the right direction."

"The Baldrige process doesn't guarantee financial prosperity, but it puts you on the right track," Malandrakis continues. "There are many other outside influences, such as economic conditions, but it sure is a valuable tool to any business competing to survive and to be the best in its class."

Cooperation between companies is one way to help assure that survival, and it's one of the most striking benefits of the Baldrige process, according to Malandrakis. "We want to share what we learn through the Baldrige process with other companies," he says. "At one time, companies wouldn't share information. But the Baldrige has helped in the communication arena, where firms like Xerox, Motorola, and Perkin-Elmer are now talking to one another on a complementary-type basis and sharing ideas.

"Today, it is not only the individual company that is forced to become more competitive: The whole American industry has been forced to become more competitive with foreign competition. The Baldrige process has fostered a spirit of cooperation between American companies that I don't think would have existed without it."

Preston Trucking Company

This widespread organization applied for the Baldrige two years in a row; each time it learned valuable lessons about who its customers are and how to assure them world-class quality.

"We service approximately 95 percent of the United States through quality partnerships," says Patrick J. Walsh, manager of Quality at Preston Trucking Company (Preston, MD). "We have direct operational areas that basically cover the northeast quadrant of the United States, running to the Illinois-Iowa border, down to St. Louis, MO, through the Virginias, and all the way up the east coast."

What attracted this far-reaching organization to the Baldrige process? "We wanted to accelerate our rate of improvement," Walsh replies. "The Baldrige criteria are an excellent 'blueprint' for quality."

Customer demands were another strong motivator for Preston to become involved in the Baldrige process. "Another reason we applied is that many of our customers were asking us to look at the Baldrige application criteria and to apply for the Award," he explains. "In fact, some made it a condition of doing business with them."

Award Winning Quality

Once Preston looked into the criteria, it was pleased with what it learned. "The criteria are excellent," Walsh asserts. "We view the Baldrige application as a certification to world-class quality."

THE FIRST YEAR: LESSONS TO BE LEARNED

Walsh explains that Preston has applied for the Award twice to date. While the company has yet to receive a site visit, it has received a wealth of feedback that is helping it to improve every facet of its operation. He relates the learning, growing process that Preston has gone through so far in applying for the Award:

"The first year, there was a team of four people, which included Preston's vice president of Marketing and Quality, an outside consultant, the senior vice president of Customer Service, and the director of Market Segmentation. The latter two people were in charge of gathering the data for the application.

"We had 86 locations when we applied the first time, and employed a little over 6,000 associates (employees)," Walsh recalls. "The first year, there was a lot of scrambling to gather the material because frankly, we weren't as well organized as we would have liked to be.

"The application was put together at the home office," Walsh continues. "The four people on the committee went around to each department and gathered all this information. Then the committee decided what information from each department applied to what section. Finally, the vice president of Marketing and the outside consultant wrote the application."

> **"Many of our customers were asking us to look at the Baldrige application criteria and to apply for the Award. In fact, some made it a condition of doing business with them."**

"Prior to the committee's gathering up information, everyone in each department was busy gathering information for them. Everyone was involved with trying to figure out what information might apply, such as 'what is our department doing under customer satisfaction?' There was a public bulletin board where they could post ideas and anyone could grab ideas from there. So that way, everyone could contribute. There were some interviews with department managers to clarify things and to get a little more information where needed."

What lessons did Preston learn the first time around? "The first year was very painful, because when we went through the application, we found that we were asked to provide measurements and information that just weren't there," Walsh concedes. "By that, I mean we had a lot of facts, trends, and numbers, but we had little information on *why*, and *where*, and things like that—we had a lot of data and not enough information.

"Also, we weren't completely focused on identifying root causes. That is, we weren't identifying all the critical factors that our customers wanted, both internally and externally."

LEARNING FROM EXPERIENCE THE SECOND TIME AROUND

The second time Preston applied for the Baldrige Award, the company changed the way it gathered information and wrote the Baldrige application. It was considerably more focused in its effort. "The first time we applied, there was a group of four people that did the work in a three-week period. They worked very long hours," Walsh recalls.

"The second time, however, three people gathered the facts together and wrote the application. They allowed themselves four to five weeks to do this the second time around.

"They gave us a written form. It contained specific questions for us to answer, such as what sections and what questions we needed to answer in the application. We were asked how we would answer, what we have measurements for, and what are the results of those measurements are."

> **"We didn't know who our customers were. We didn't know what they expected from us. And we didn't know whether they were satisfied. We learned all this through filling out the application."**

"They also gave us the information from our area from last year's application and asked what we are doing now in these same areas. We were asked to update the information. Basically, the same people were involved, but some of the responsibility was shifted."

Walsh points out that in filling out the application the second time, it became apparent that Preston had improved in several different areas. "We feel we've identified our markets and our customers. We know what market segments we want to go after, and what is important to the customer in selecting a carrier. We have upgraded our measurements in respect to the critical factors of what the customer wants."

HOW THE BALDRIGE IS HELPING PRESTON IMPROVE

According to Walsh, the Baldrige process has helped Preston to improve its operation in several significant ways. "First, working with the Baldrige application has given us a better understanding of where we are and who we are as a company," he explains. "Second, going after the Baldrige has helped us improve our processes,

which has helped our bottom line."

In addition to these factors, the Baldrige process is helping Preston improve its operations in the following significant areas, Walsh reports:

◆ **Customer awareness.** The Baldrige application process has helped Preston to uncover weaknesses in its customer service function. "We found out that one of our weak points was customer satisfaction," Walsh concedes. "We didn't know who our customers were. We didn't know what they expected from us. And we didn't know whether they were satisfied.

"We learned all this through both years of filling out the application. Once we recognized where we needed to improve, we hired an outside marketing firm to survey our customers, and used focus groups to get the information we needed. We used the results to restructure our organization to service our customers more efficiently."

How did the Baldrige help Preston identify these factors? "Just answering the questions is a help," replies Walsh. "When the questions specifically ask you what sort of measurements you used or what things your customers are looking for and you can't answer because you don't have the information that says, 'This is what our customers want,' you know you have a problem," he asserts. "The first year we applied, we found that we couldn't do that."

◆ **Establishing a sound, universal management process.** "Our whole quality process and our management process are inseparable—our management process is universally deployed at Preston Trucking Company," says Walsh. "In order to manage at Preston, we manage according to the fundamentals of performance management. We now know that our manager in Portland, Maine, manages exactly the same way as the manager in Peoria, Illinois.

"Our management process is based on four key concepts," explains Walsh. These concepts are the following:

❶ *You have to pinpoint specifically what you want your people to do.*

❷ *You have to be able to measure it.*

❸ *You have to provide feedback to your people so that they know how they are doing.*

❹ *You have to apply the consequences—good or bad.*

"We are more interested in reinforcing the positive outcomes rather than the negative consequences," Walsh notes.

◆ **Coordinating the training and team efforts**

companywide. "With so many sites, training is difficult and costly," Walsh admits. "We conduct product knowledge training, leadership training, quality freight handling training, hazardous materials and safety training, etc.—but [before the Baldrige process] we didn't have our training *structured*.

"Furthermore, we didn't know who had been through what training and when. We have used outside consultants for training, but most recently, we have brought all our training in-house.

"Team training has become an important factor," Walsh adds. "We now have a lot of self-managed teams in our home office. The key areas where we run into problems are still the 86 locations. How can we get everybody working as a team at all these locations? We now know we need to train our associates and give them the tools they need to act as teams in all our locations."

◆ **Enhancing communications throughout the organization.** To get its many locations going in the same direction at the same time, Preston has "implemented various ways of communicating with our associates," says Walsh.

For example, Preston promotes its suggestion process in its company newspaper. "Our newspaper is considered a 'celebration' magazine," Walsh explains. "It announces who achieved what, when, where, and how. We celebrate any time management or associates meet the goals they have set."

IT'S NOT THE WINNING, IT'S THE PROCESS

All in all, Walsh gives the Baldrige press high marks as a quality improvement tool. "We have complete confidence in the effectiveness of the application. It does help an organization to improve itself.

"We also highly recommend to other companies that they at least fill out the application. If they don't want to apply, they should at least go through the process of filling out the application for the purposes of self-assessment.

"After all, winning the Award isn't the most important aspect of the process—it's the *process itself* that matters," Walsh points out. "The Award is a by-product; it is something incidental that you might get. It's the *process* that helps you improve."

> "We have complete confidence in the effectiveness of the application—it does help an organization to improve itself. Winning the Award isn't the most important aspect of the process—it's the process itself that matters. It's the process that helps you improve."

"We will use Baldrige criteria again this year, but we will not apply. However, we will be applying again for the Baldrige Award in the future," he adds.

Even without the Award, it's clear that Preston is going a long way toward satisfying both its external and internal customers. "We were listed in *The 100 Best Companies to Work for in America*," reports Walsh. "We are concerned about our people, and we feel that our quality process is strong and alive at all our 86 locations."

Rockwell International Corp.

This company's Baldrige-inspired Total Customer Satisfaction process identifies five key areas for strengthening customer awareness and responsiveness.

Since 1983, Rockwell International Corporation's Digital Communications Division, or DCD (Newport Beach, CA), has been involved in a successful continuous quality improvement effort. Instrumental in its recent efforts have been the criteria set out by the Malcolm Baldrige National Quality Award.

"We became involved with the Baldrige the first year it was announced," reports Lee Troxler, division director of Quality. "It provides a very effective way for us to assess ourselves."

BALDRIGE BREEDS ROCKWELL'S TOTAL CUSTOMER SATISFACTION PROCESS

By studying Baldrige criteria, the DCD has been able to identify five specific areas in which to concentrate some of its efforts. These fall under the umbrella of its Total Customer Satisfaction (TCS) process, which covers the following topics:

✱ **The importance of service improvement and the internal customer.** "One of the first things we realized about the Baldrige criteria was that they addressed a lot more than just *product* quality and *external* customers," says Troxler. "In the past, we had concentrated heavily on these two areas." However, the criteria helped the DCD realize that it needed to focus some of its efforts on *service* quality and *internal* customers.

✱ **Training in all aspects of quality.** Part of this expansion of thought has been accomplished through the TCS training program. To date, over 1,100 employees in the DCD have received training that focuses on the internal customer concept, service quality, and other Baldrige criteria.

"The training helps employees improve their processes so that they can improve their results to internal customers," explains Troxler. "This will ultimately help to improve service to external customers."

Quite unexpectedly, the training (which is cross-functional) has had another benefit. "After their training, employees report that they have gotten to know employees in other departments much better," states Eileen Algaze, public relations manager, who herself participated in the training. "Now they talk to one another a lot more, understand one another's problems, and work better together."

In other words, the training helped to break down the "functional silos" (for an explanation of functional silos, see the section on Motorola, Chapter Two) that so often separate departments from one another. "The training really 'warmed the environment' here and opened up communication," says Algaze.

"There is more of a feeling that we're all in this together. We work as a team now, not as individual departments."

✱ **Application of training principles.** Since the training, the emphasis has been on applying the training principles on the job, particularly in key areas. Among these are cycle time reduction and administrative support.

"We are mapping our processes so that we can look at each step and identify the internal customers," states Troxler. "Then we can reduce the cycle time of the processes."

✱ **Executive management council.** TCS is managed by an executive management council, chaired by Troxler. The council meets monthly to review progress and identify future goals based on the input it receives.

Award Winning Quality

> "One of the first things we realized about the Baldrige criteria was that they addressed a lot more than just <u>product</u> quality and <u>external</u> customers." The criteria helped the DCD realize that it needed to focus some of its efforts on <u>service</u> quality and <u>internal</u> customers.

"For example, we recently completed a survey of our major U.S. customers," reports Troxler. "We plan to review the results of this survey and create an action plan to resolve any key issues that it identifies."

✮ **Quality teams.** As issues are identified, the council appoints teams to address them. Some teams are *ad hoc;* others are *continuous. Ad hoc* teams work on one-time issues that can be resolved with closure.

Continuous teams work on ongoing issues. An example is customer action teams, which pair DCD representatives with customer representatives to address ways to continually improve performance and communication.

▶ *Customer Team in Action* ➤ Troxler cites an example of the formation of a customer action team. "We had one customer that was returning parts they said were defective," he notes. However, DCD retesting showed that approximately 60 percent of the "rejects" were testing well. DCD tried to explain this to the customer, but the customer initially did not want to work with the DCD on resolving the issue.

"Finally, they agreed to participate with us," Troxler continues. By working together, the two companies found a number of things that each could do to improve performance and communication. "The customer is now a strong advocate of the team concept, and they actually lead it," he states. "In fact, when new products come out, the customer contacts us so that we can work together on them."

COMMITMENT TO QUALITY THROUGH BALDRIGE PAYS OFF

The DCD's commitment to quality and its use of Baldrige criteria for self-assessment has really benefited the Division, reports Troxler. On one product line,

for example, the DCD has been able to realize the following improvements:

> **"The training really 'warmed the environment' here and opened up communication. There is more of a feeling that we're all in this together. We work as a team now, not as individual departments."**

➤ Reduce the defect rate by a factor of 10 (from approximately 1,000 ppm to under 100 ppm).

➤ Reduce customer rejects by 100 percent.

➤ Improve throughput time by roughly 400 percent.

➤ Improve reliability by a factor of 20 (allowing it to extend its warranty to 5 years).

➤ Improve gross profits despite a price reduction.

With results like these, the DCD is confident that its commitment to using the Baldrige process as a quality tool is paying off in a big way.

Texas Instruments Inc.

The Baldrige process is helping this industry leader design a plan to assure that the entire organization fulfills its promise to "do it right the first time."

Since its infancy, Texas Instruments Inc. (Dallas) has been synonymous with quality. So it's no surprise that when the nation's leading-edge companies began their journeys toward continuous quality improvement in the early 1980s, TI was up there among the leaders.

"We have always had an aggressive quality improvement strategy," says Mike Cooney, vice president and Defense Systems and Electronics Group manager of Quality and Reliability Assurance. "Our management team attended Crosby College and has been through Juran training. As a result, we felt we had the tools we needed and were well on our way toward quality improvement, using the road map we set for ourselves in the early 1980s."

Cooney explains that TI's quality improvement efforts revolve around three cornerstones:

❶ **Customer focus**

❷ **Continuous improvement**

❸ **Employee involvement**

Rather than being separate efforts, these three cornerstones are integrated into the company's business objectives, strategies, tactics, and management styles. In addition, says Cooney, quality improvement efforts permeate *the entire organization*, not just the manufacturing function. Managers in all departments and at all levels receive training in how to utilize quality principles in their daily decision-making activities.

QUALITY IN ACTION: A POLICY BACKED BY QUALITY INITIATIVES

To reinforce TI's commitment to excellence, copies of the company's quality policy are posted throughout the facilities. This policy states:

"For every product or service we offer, we will understand the requirements that meet the customers' needs, and we will conform to those requirements without exception. For every job each TIer performs, the performance standard is **DO IT RIGHT THE FIRST TIME.***"*

This quality pledge applies to internal customers as well as external customers, Cooney notes.

To implement this policy throughout its organization, the Defense Systems and Electronics Group

> **"The Baldrige showed us that we could benchmark our processes against almost _any_ electronics manufacturer. That is, if you dissect an electronic product, the processes tend to be similar, regardless of the product being made."**

(DS&EG) launched a number of initiatives:

Award Winning Quality

■ **Effectiveness teams** (similar to quality circles) were created in 1984. These teams are organized by discipline and are given the responsibility to make process improvements.

■ **Cell teams** are composed of representatives from various departments and make improvements designed to provide better integration among multiple functions.

■ **Customer visits.** DS&EG encourages customers to visit its facilities and offer direct feedback to DS&EG employees on their work. Conversely, the Group sends its employees to customer locations to see their products in action.

■ **Attitude surveys.** The Group has a number of initiatives designed to promote and encourage employee involvement. One of these is an annual attitude survey that covers a wide range of issues, including whether employees understand the quality requirements of their jobs (a question which close to 95 percent of DS&EG employees have answered in the affirmative).

THE BALDRIGE PROCESS—A TOOL FOR MEASURING QUALITY PROGRESS

In spite of all the successful quality efforts it deployed in the early to mid-1980s, DS&EG still lacked an effective set of criteria by which to measure its progress. "We needed some criteria to let us know that we were on course and that our strategy was still driving us in the right direction," reports Cooney.

When the Baldrige Award was introduced in 1987, DS&EG management realized that the Award provided that set of criteria. "We began to measure and assess ourselves using the Baldrige criteria to see where we were," Cooney reports.

"Then we began to conduct some internal training using the criteria as guidelines." One of the Group's staff members was selected as a Baldrige examiner. As such, he was selected to conduct the Group's training.

In 1988/89, DS&EG had each of its businesses and functional organizations write "miniapplications" based on the Baldrige criteria, formatting these applications just like the Baldrige application.

THE PURSUIT OF THE BALDRIGE BRINGS INVALUABLE FEEDBACK

By 1990, the Group felt it was far enough along in its improvement efforts to make a formal application for the Baldrige Award. It made the first cut, but did not receive a site visit.

However, feedback from the Baldrige examiners proved invaluable. "The Baldrige feedback gave us an independent look at our strategies and road map," explains Cooney. "It not only confirmed some things that we already knew needed improvement but also gave us insight into some areas where we had previously been narrowly focused."

The feedback was particularly helpful in the following areas:

◆ **Benchmarking.** Previously, DS&EG had benchmarked its processes principally with competitors in the defense electronics industry. "The Baldrige showed us that we could benchmark our processes against almost *any* electronics manufacturer," Cooney says. "That is, if you dissect an electronic product, the processes tend to be similar, regardless of the product

being made."

◆ **Goal-setting.** The Group had been setting its goals and measuring itself against its direct competition. Again, the Baldrige showed that it should set its goals around the best in any market.

> "The Baldrige feedback gave us an independent look at our strategies and road map. It not only confirmed some things that we already knew needed improvement but also gave us insight into some areas where we had previously been narrowly focused."

Using the feedback it received from the 1990 Baldrige assessment, a DS&EG management committee identified and pursued five improvement efforts for 1991. "We reapplied for the Award in 1991 and received a site visit," Cooney points out. He adds that the Group plans to study last year's Baldrige feedback report along with its own feedback assessment to design its quality action plan for the coming year.

Whether TI wins the Award this year, the Baldrige process will continue to help the company learn, grow, and advance in its quest to deliver top-quality products and services to its customers.

Conclusion

The Bottom Line:
Continuous Improvement Is What Counts

As you've learned from reading the comprehensive success stories detailed in this book, achieving award winning quality is a painstaking process. It takes a tremendous amount of commitment and dedication to achieve the level of excellence that fulfills the stringent Malcolm Baldrige National Quality Award criteria, and also to apply for the Award.

Yet every year, thousands and thousands of companies request applications, and dozens of them actually apply for the Award, some going through the difficult application process year after year.

Why do so many companies undertake this monumental effort? Some are encouraged to apply by their customers, who want to do business with only the most quality-effective suppliers. But as this book illustrates, most companies that participate in the Baldrige process do so with one critical goal in mind: *self-improvement*.

The Baldrige application process—and even the Award itself—will certainly not solve all a company's problems. It is not a panacea, and should never be regarded as such. However, it *is* a sound, thorough blueprint for quality improvement, and it has stimulated interest in quality in the United States as nothing has ever done before. The Baldrige process is helping to bring U.S. companies together to pool their ideas, resources, and strategies for keeping their industries strong and viable.

The bottom line is this: The companies that benefit most from the Baldrige process are the ones that recognize that it's not winning the Award that counts the most; it's developing the discipline, drive, and vision to set their organizations on the path to excellence, and then to keep striving ever onward toward continuous improvement. As Roy Bauer of IBM Rochester says, "People need to think of applying for the Baldrige as secondary. The benefits from doing the self-assessment are what *really* count."

Also, true quality winners never rest on their laurels: They recognize that improvement doesn't stop with receiving a Baldrige Award—or any other award, for that matter: It must be an *ongoing* process that never ends. Ron Schmidt of Zytec Corporation expresses it this way: "[Winning the Baldrige] is kind of a wayside rest in our journey. We're going to stop and smell the roses a little bit, but then we're going right back out on the road, because we know we have a lot of improvement to do yet."

Christian Witzke of Marlow Industries agrees: "The voyage continues; the Award was just a milestone along the way. Every year, the competition gets stiffer, and your customers' requirements increase. Therefore, every year, you need to keep improving if you are to maintain—or even better, *improve*—your position in your industry."

This commitment to continuous improvement is crucial if your company is to survive—and *thrive*—in today's challenging marketplace. Putting the powerful Baldrige process to work as an improvement tool can help your own organization to be a quality winner.

Notes